EVERY [illegible] T

EVERY SINGLE MOMENT:

The Best Way to Handle Singleness in the Wait

ANTONIA NAZOMBE

ISBN-13: 978-99908-0-775-2

Cover Design by Watipaso Kaliwo

DEDICATION

To every woman, you are deeply loved and cherished by God

PREFACE

There is a recurring message of marriage in seminars, on social media, and in conversations that show that marriage is a burning issue in this generation. I've personally witnessed and participated in conversations with other women dominated by the discourse on relationships, dating, courting and marriage. The preoccupation with dating, relationships, marriage, and courting suggests that this is the most pressing concern, especially, among unmarried women. The pressure for women to get married has been propelled by the society at large, including the church. While this pressure may arise from good intentions, it usually causes a lot of discomfort and frustration among unmarried women. There are women who have embraced the idea of marriage and are aware of its possibilities. However, they are experiencing a prolonged season of singleness because they haven't met their life partners. For these women, even the mention of a hypothetical future husband or marriage can be cause for too much thought and anxiety. For this reason, you find a lot of women stressed over, looking, waiting and praying for their potential husband.

I found myself bothered by the level of anxiety unmarried women had over their marital future and my heart was moved to wonder: "How could a single woman, who believes she is ready for marriage remain present to her singleness without neglecting her aspirations to be married?" To be honest, living in one reality while desiring the other could be tricky. It can have a push and pull effect on you. You could easily thrust yourself into the future through planning and imagining your ideal life as a married woman, meeting your spouse, etc. And when you remember that you shouldn't jump ahead of yourself, you would have to drag yourself to the present and try and embrace your singleness. *A push and pull.* So how do you survive this crucial period of singleness that could either make you or break you? How could you avoid falling into doubt and shame?

This book is a compilation of my thoughts, experiences, and lessons as a single Christian lady and prospective wife. I hope in sharing my perspective, lessons, and experiences you will find content that will prove to be useful to your own journey. Ultimately, my desire is that you navigate your season of waiting guided by the peace of God and thrive in the middle, filled with godly expectation and without hoarding any bitterness, jealousy or anger. My prayer is that when you come out on the other side of your season you would arrive with no regrets. May, you be uplifted by every word. Enjoy reading!

Xoxo,

Antonia

CONTENTS

CONTENTS

CHAPTER ONE

GOD IS LOVE

This is love: not that we loved God, but that he loved us and sent his Son as an atoning sacrifice for our sin.

1 John 4:10

Love is a core aspect of God's character and nature. God's love stems from his being and he extends it to everyone without partiality. God decided before the foundations of the earth to love us.[1] There is no greater love that you will ever know. Knowing God means responding to his love. The purest and truest love there is. If you think you've experienced love and it was outside of God, then you, haven't known true love. However, if that is your case, take heart, this is your chance to know the greatest love of all and you, my friend are in for the best ride of your life. This love is like no other.

When I was fourteen years old in my second year of high school, I was so frustrated about these "relationship things" and I really wanted to know the true meaning of love as regards boy-girl relationships. I was newly saved at the time and I had been told that the Bible had the solutions to all life problems. In my frustration, I set out to look for advice on love from the Bible (the wisest decision I have ever made).

I was not familiar with the Bible, so I turned to the concordance and looked up the word, love and took note of the referenced verses. You might have already guessed with which verse I began my search, John

3:16. I read it but I was not satisfied because it did not depict the type of love I was looking for. I read the rest of the verses listed in the index and the result was the same each time. However, one verse stood out to me from all of the verses I'd read. It was John 15:13. Yet, it still made no sense to me. This actually increased my frustration again, because I wasn't seeking out that kind of love. All I wanted to know was whether that specific boy at the time loved me or not and if I should date him or not. Instead, the Scriptures were uncovering something rather peculiar about love and it concerned someone dying for his friends! Can you all relate? I honestly wasn't looking for something THAT serious! BUT there was something beautiful that happened at that moment. The Holy Spirit gently whispered words that unleashed new truths to my very limited understanding at the time. He sweetly told me, "That's what love is". I was stunned! My arguments were immediately silenced. It is one of my most memorable revelations. I began to piece together everything I'd known and heard about love up to that point in my life and somehow, it made perfect sense that true love stemmed only from God. My thinking about love shifted and I was taken on a whole new journey.

THIS IS LOVE

John 15:13 reads, "*Greater love has no one than this: to lay down one's life for one's friends.*" This verse gets me every time. It's not just love but "greater love." **No one has!** Not your mum, not your dad, not your boyfriend, not your brother or sister and not even your best friend. None of these dear people would willingly lay down their lives for you especially when you don't deserve it. God loved us whilst we were still sinners (Romans 5:8) and his love was fully demonstrated when he sent his only son Jesus Christ to die on the cross for our sins paying the debt that we owed.

You may be wondering what this has do to with singleness. It has everything to do with it. You are God's beloved. You were created to be loved without reservation. The cross demonstrates that the greatest love of all was fully poured out for you. As you are seeking out love, you need to know what love looks like. And the only way you could get to know true love is if you look to the cross. I literally mean get soaked in the

Scriptures and study about the love of God towards mankind. Your understanding of love should stem from God and the love he demonstrated by sending his only Son to die for your sins. It will make all the difference.

You may be thinking along the same lines as I did, "I just want a man" or "I just want to know if I am ever going to get married." Before you go looking for love from another human being, know that you are perfectly loved by God. Understand that true love and satisfaction can only be found in him. It's the perfect love [2]that Jesus has bestowed on us which empowers us to love ourselves and to love others (including your future spouse). You could genuinely render love to another person only when you have known and received the love Christ has for you. This book won't offer you a quick fix to help you find Mr. Right but the information in here will be worthwhile. As you learn more about God's heart for you, you'll begin to experience freedom over every anxiety that arises as a result of your singleness.

LOVE AWARE

God loves you. He loves you as an individual. Not you as part of your church group, your city or your family. He particularly loves you. Don't brush it off as something you've heard one too many times. You've got to recognise and take hold of this truth. Jesus died for the whole world and he also specifically died for you. Receiving this love for yourself will have a great impact on your life. *Jesus loves me,* will no longer be a meaningless mantra but a truth you are actually living out. The Bible in 1 John 4:16 (MSG) says, "*we know it so well, we've embraced it heart and soul, this love that comes from God.*" Know the love of God so well that even if you don't emotionally "feel" loved, you are still sure of his love for you. Become convinced of God's love for you, "embrace it, heart and soul."

You cannot determine God's love for you by pulling out petals off a rose. In particular, I like the Amplified version of the same verse (1 John 4:16) it says, "*and we know (understand, recognize, are conscious of by observation and by experience and believe [adhere to and put faith in and rely on the love God cherishes for us...*" The Amplified, expounds on the word "*know*" using additional words— "recognise," and "are conscious of by observation." In the morning when you wake up, be conscious of God's love for you, watch for his love throughout the day, deliberately recognising his acts of love. Don't be ignorant in certain situations when you witness an unusual and good occurrence towards you and brush it off as a coincidence or pure luck when it is a demonstration of God's love.

Paul said in Ephesians 3: 17b- 19, *"...and I pray, you being rooted and established in love may have power, together with God's holy people to grasp how wide and long and deep is the love of Christ, and to know the love that surpasses-knowledge that you may be filled to the measure of all the fullness of God."* The love of God is not logical. No one can really comprehend the kind of love that's affectionate towards sinners. You may have symptoms in your life that you feel disqualify you of love, let alone God's love. As you become more established in God's love, you will no longer rely on your senses to signify just how loved you are. It's mind-blowing to know that it is the process of knowing God's love for you that will lead you to experience a deeper life in Christ.

SELF-LOVE

When you grasp the new revelation of God's love for you that has been relayed, above, you will be ushered into a better understanding of who you are—his Beloved. Identifying as his beloved will shape your understanding of self-love and it's simple: Self-love is having a Christ-like love for yourself. Inspired by his love for you, the Lord also wants you to love yourself. *"Love your neighbour as you love yourself"*[3]. In most cases, this verse has been interpreted with the bold assumption that each individual possesses self-love. I know from personal experience that it can be easier to say mean and hurtful things to yourself than to someone else. I have certainly been at the forefront of criticising myself. One day, as I was being cruel to myself, I realised that there was no-one else present with me on whom I could place the blame of influencing the self-degrading thoughts. I was solely responsible for demeaning myself.

Sometimes you may feel justified to give yourself a scolding for a mistake you made. And as you treat yourself harshly you may think God supports your actions. Nothing could be further from the truth. God is not at any point in agreement with you when you speak unkind words to yourself. That's you, all on your own accepting the devil's negative suggestions about you. God has already made up his mind about you. He has distinguished you as—**worthy of love**.

Now, *you* need to begin to believe it. You are the one who looks in the mirror and sees an undesirable reflection. Also, I am sure that you have at one time, singled yourself out as less beautiful from a group photograph. Honey, what God wants for you is to look into that mirror and like what you see. You need to fix your glasses. It's not the image that has a problem but rather your view. No outfit will ever look good on you if you already have a distorted image of yourself. Resolve that you will embrace yourself as you are.

Self-hatred will inflict a lot of damage to your soul. You cannot state all the things you hate about yourself and expect to treat yourself well. You say, "I hate my nose, I hate my life; I hate...I hate...I hate..." How about you begin to state what you love about yourself. God has loved you in spite of your inadequacies. Living in this truth will help you embrace the parts of you that you don't like. You need to conform to the new way of life where you speak lovely and life-giving words to yourself. Instead of saying, "I hate my nose declare, "I have a perfect nose." Heck, my nose does the job! That's good enough for me. You can do this anytime hateful thoughts arise within you, it also helps to quote appropriate Scripture to strengthen your affirmation. It may not happen overnight but eventually, you will conform to God's lifestyle of love.

If you are to love others well; you need to firstly work on loving yourself. Taking the lead in loving yourself means that you shouldn't wait for validation from other people to determine your self-worth. We all crave praise—especially from people we admire. Being appreciated is great but you shouldn't live off of other people's compliments. Caring too much about what others think of you becomes an impediment to how you view yourself. When you don't possess any self-esteem, you allow people to define your worth. Once you place your worth in other people's hands, you give them the freedom to decide how to treat you. So if your value to someone is 50% then they give you 50% worth of treatment and you begin to believe that's your worth. If you are lucky some will rate you as the precious gem that you are but I wouldn't be surprised if most people placed insignificant worth on you.

This is especially important for women because men prey on insecure women. They know how to spot them. They take one look at you and notice when everything about you reeks of timidity. You would agree with me that you've observed certain relationships and asked yourself, "How did she end up with a guy like that?" This guy, who is probably overbearing, unkind and very controlling and the girl who is overly compliant. The question that usually follows is, "Why is she still with him?" My heart truly beaks over the women who are in toxic relationships with men who do not love or respect them. It always seems like everyone around them knows this man is not good for them apart from the woman herself. Clearly, one mustn't have known real love to accept cheap and worthless counterfeits of love. If you practice self-love you would steer clear of anything and anyone who seeks to harm you. May this serve as a reminder when you have doubts about your worth: God has given all his love to you fully aware of the human being that you are, flaws and all.

AM I THE ONLY ONE?

Loving God, letting God love you, loving yourself and loving others. Love demands so much from us. It really isn't as simple as 1, 2, 3 but it is possible. By now, you know that becoming united with the love of your life is not as simple as you may have imagined and preferred. For some, you've been waiting for years and you are not so young anymore. And maybe for you my sister, it hasn't been that long since you became interested in getting married. Yet, you have an intense longing for marriage and so, it feels like years since you've been waiting. Both situations are equally valid.

Before going any further I want you to just pause for a minute, take a deep breath, and reckon within yourself that *you* have made the deliberate *decision* to involve God in your love affairs. It is okay, to smile or even cry because this is a brave thing you have done. It is God honouring and you ought to applaud yourself for it. Well done!

I understand singleness can feel weighty. I know the number of times I've hoped to discover a formula that would resolve my queries. Have you ever wished that life would offer you clues that would lead you straight into the arms of your loved one? Well, you can't skip the process of waiting— as the saying goes, good things take time. Although it may not be an easy road for you, it is one you still have to take. Some of you have probably been on a couple of blind dates set up by your friends or relatives; maybe you linked up with professional matchmakers or tried online dating but nothing seems to work. You've probably asked yourself and wondered why you are still trying. More so, why you are still trying God's way.

God's way demands that you literally go in blind and fully trust him. I know I've definitely found myself at wit's end, wondering why I should keep upholding God's way when my friends are not honouring God as singles or in their relationships; yet things still seem to be working out for them. Many are the times I've felt maybe it is not a big deal anymore to put God first in all our affairs including our relationships. I've felt alone on this path. I once, literally uttered to the Lord, "Am I the only one?" The answer I received from the Lord was based on 2 Kings 6:13-16 (make it a point to read the Scripture). I was reminded of this truth, "If you ever feel you are the only one, remember there are more with you than those that are with the world." These words bring me so much comfort.

How exciting it is to know that you are not alone! As a matter of fact, you are the one who has made the better decision by putting your trust in the Lord and not following the world. "There are more with us." You are on the winning team. You may be surrounded by the world with its loud opinions and philosophies about dating, marriage, and purity. But because your ways are the ways of the Lord, you have the upper hand and you have heaven cheering you on. No, worldly opinion can stand against heaven!

Do you know what is in store for you because of this great decision to follow the Lord? The Bible in Proverbs 18:10 says, *"The name of the LORD is a strong tower and the righteous runneth into it and are safe."* In Christ, you are protected from an endless list of possible bad happenings including, disease, unnecessary heartbreak, and unplanned pregnancies. You basically have an easier lifestyle because you've got God's covering over. As you depend and trust in him, he takes care of you. When you flee compromise and uphold the Lord's ways, you are safe in him. How amazing is that?

Now that you are sure that you are on the right track, let's forge on ahead to overcome any obstacles on your journey, so that at the end of the day you are single and also, whole. In addition to that, you will be among the women who are planning and preparing for the future not from a place of defeat but with gladness.

CHAPTER TWO

WHEN GOD AWAKENS YOUR DESIRES

The desire of the righteous ends only in good

Proverbs 11:23

Has the thought of marriage become a hidden desire that you've stowed away in the deep corners of your heart? I think of people like Gideon and the Shunammite woman from the Bible. These two people were both lacking in some capacity— Gideon came from the weakest clan in Manasseh and the Shunammite woman was childless. One thing that is significant in both stories is that when presented with a solution for their predicament, they were both doubtful. When the Shunammite woman was told that she would have the son she had yearned for, she objected saying: *"No, my Lord! Please, man of God, don't mislead your servant!"*[1] And the following was Gideon's reaction: *"Pardon me, my lord, but how can I save Israel? My clan is the weakest in Manasseh and I am the least in my family"*[2]

Every woman has a beautiful innate desire to get married, one day. When you were younger, you, probably dreamt of walking down the aisle with the love of your life by a certain age but sometimes things don't always go according to plan. You could easily bury your initial desire for marriage under shame, fear, and defeat from this unfulfilled dream. Even you could react like Gideon and the Shunammite woman when you come across Scripture like Psalm 37:4, that says, *"Delight in the LORD and he will give you the desires of your heart."* This wouldn't make sense to someone who feels forsaken.

I believe God places desires in our hearts that he wants to fulfil in our lives. These desires are usually different from what we would have imagined for ourselves and the default option for most people is to subdue these inclinations. It is possible to function for years without these feelings ever resurfacing. Sometimes our hopes for good things seem overly ambitious. If we are honest with ourselves the reality of those desires ever taking form might seem impossible, so it's easier to put it off because it hurts too much to believe that it would happen. However, you would agree with me that these God-given desires always resurface. God deliberately reminds you of these desires! Why? Because he put them on the inside of you and he wants you to look to him for the fulfilment of these dreams.

Looking to God for the fulfilment of your heart desires involves waiting. Sometimes, waiting on God can take you on a rollercoaster ride that starts off, hopeful and expectant and then eventually turns into hopelessness and despair. The moments you despair and feel hopeless are very crucial because once you become discouraged, it is easy to convince yourself into actualising your desires by your own efforts. Now, that's setting yourself up for disaster. I definitely learnt this the hard way and I believe this topic is worth exploring.

LESSONS FROM ABRAHAM

We get to learn from Abraham's journey of faith. This part of the story of Abram (before God changed his name to Abraham) is found in Genesis, chapters, 12 -16. God awoke a hidden desire in Abram. When God called Abram at the age of 75, he and his wife, Sarai, 65, were childless. As you may have deduced, at that age, Abram and Sarai should have been expecting grandchildren. Even for Bible times, Abram and Sarai were way past the childbearing age. At around the same time, Abram was called, God made a promise to him and his wife Sarai that they would have the child that they had desperately been wanting for years.

However, it took twenty-five years from the time God made a promise to Abram up until the time Abram would actually get to hold the child of the promise in his arms. You will agree with me that twenty-five years is a long time and it's quite enough time for one to grow impatient during the period of waiting. The wait was hectic for Abraham and Sarai. At a certain point Abram got so frustrated he asked God for a sign (Genesis 15). Abram did this because God had continued to reveal more promises to him about the descendants he would have in the future yet at *that* moment Abram still had no child. Ten years after the time that God had made the promise, desperation arose within Abram and Sarai as they awaited the fulfilment of the promise. Filled with anxiety that she would never be a mother, Sarai gave Abram her slave girl, Hagar, to be his wife so that Hagar would bear Abram a child (Genesis 16). Indeed Hagar conceived and bore Abram a son, Ishmael, but he was not the son of the promise.

I find it fascinating that up until the time God had promised Abram that he would be a father there is no record in the Bible of him and his wife previously considering other methods of conception. They were living a normal life as a childless couple. They had learnt to live with a suppressed desire probably because they felt hopeless. Yet, when God reminded Abram and Sarai of their heart's desire and when God showed interest in fulfilling that desire, this couple became rather discomposed. All their frustrations that had been hidden for so long now became exposed.

I am imagining this for you as a woman who has reached a suitable age for marriage. You are open to a being in a relationship that will lead to marriage. However, years are passing by but your significant other is nowhere in sight. On top of that, you have prayed about it and you know God is for you and he has confirmed with his peace that he is bringing someone your way. However, nothing seems to be changing, I bet you would also get frustrated.

WHEN DESPERATION KICKS IN

The story of Abraham and Sarah conveys that desperation reveals itself in its fullest when there is a possibility that our hidden desires could become true as was the case here. This would definitely be relevant to a woman who is aware of the possibility of marriage but unsure of it. Especially as time goes by and the desire has yet to be fulfilled; you begin to examine your current state with its many flaws. For example, I am getting older, I am about to finish college and I don't have a boyfriend, all the guys that come my way are disappointing, etc. This self-examination leaches worry into the situation and enhances your desperation.

As a result, you doubt God and take matters into your own hands. It never ends well when you choose to apply your own efforts to godly matters. A lot of single women find themselves wandering—because your heart is unsettled you are always searching trying to find your "man".

I'm going, to be honest with you by telling you about my own "wandering" experience. I definitely had a lot of moments when I would walk into a room full of people and look around wondering if my future husband was present there. But there was one time when I thought God had given this one guy. He was a guy from my church who I'd recently met. I was so sure that this guy was "God-given" and by the end of that week, I had already planned our life together! I would be different around him, sometimes laugh a little harder while chatting with my friends just to be noticed. I bet he probably thought I was strange. I had gone way ahead of myself and it was unhealthy for me and probably for him too. I also marvel now about what I did back then. However, I realised that it was not about him, he was only the unfortunate individual who became a victim of my unchecked desire. It was more about me and how I had come to the conclusion that he was the "one" and I had assigned myself the responsibility of making him notice me. I tried so hard to get his attention, I acted unlike myself but I thank God that I caught myself in time before it had gone too far.

It's very unfair when you place expectations on someone who is not your future husband simply because you think he is the "one." For instance, vetting every ideal man as your potential husband and proceeding to disqualify him if he doesn't meet your standards is an unhealthy obsession. It is equally unacceptable to keep tabs on him (whether in person or online) because he is your crush. It's important that you know: even you, Christian lady, will be attracted to someone who you might not end up with. Just because you have feelings for someone at a time when you are open to marriage does not signify that he will be your husband. I remember I began to freak-out (referring to the same guy I previously told you about) after I had lost interest in him. I worried that I would be stuck with him for the rest of my life so I started backing out as if I had initially been forced to commit. It became clear to me that this had all been in my head when God told me, "I'm not asking anything of you." Finally, I could breathe easy again. I had obviously misread the situation and I was fighting a battle I had started all on my own.

This may sound ironic but, the best time to stay calm is when you feel the most desperate. When your mind is running wild, demanding that you do something about your situation. That is the best moment to stop, think and act with deliberation. Like Abraham, you risk bringing about an unwanted outcome if you act frantically.

I am hoping for you, child of God that you would rest in the promise of God to you. He is always on time. The Bible says, *"The Lord is not slow in keeping his promise as some understand slowness"* (see 2 Peter 3:9). You would agree with me that Abraham and Sarah considered God slow and now, you may also be doubting God's sense of urgency concerning your future marriage. Yet God's intentions towards you are good. Delight in him, find your pleasure in him and he will give you the desires of your heart. Leave the analysing and calculating to God. When the time comes it will happen.

I heard a minister say, "God does not dangle a carrot in front of you"[3]. You have not placed our hope in a cruel God who makes promises to his children for the fun of it. God is not setting you up to fail. He will fulfil your God-given dream for marriage. Our God is faithful.

TRUST GOD'S TIMING

For some the phrase, "God's time is the best time," may sound like a cliché. Yet, the truth of this statement remains. We rush through life trying to get to the next milestone. Now, it's marriage and next, it will be having children. While waiting on God, it may seem your situation is not changing and it's taking too long for you to meet your life partner. Because you feel delayed, you start wishing time would speed up. This is where it goes wrong for most because you resort to devising methods that would make the process shorter and more convenient for you. However, the easy way out usually becomes risky especially in the things of God. There are just no short cuts with God. Cutting corners would only delay you from reaching your intended goal because you will always end up back at square one until you take the path of the Lord's choosing.

Everyone goes through certain things in life for a reason. Sometimes, it's to train and equip you with valid lessons that will be essential to achieving your destiny. At other times, God puts time between you and your dream, to cultivate your faith. Not once has he ever put the time in between your journey and destination with intentions to harm you or as a method to keep you from realising your dream. It is always for your good. You are the one who benefits from the whole process.

Therefore, don't rush the process. There are ladies who compromise their faith and morality because they don't want to wait. There is a good chance, you will end up hurt when you compromise. Avoid self -sabotage that would ruin your God-ordained destiny. Don't try to get it done on your own; *wait* for God's best. A woman is pregnant nine months for a reason—each day, week and month contributes to the baby's development, you could ruin the baby's healthy development if you induce birth before the nine months are completed. In the same way, Child of God, don't try and rush the process. In due time your desire will be fulfilled.

Like Abraham and Sarah, you may get weary while you are waiting. But consider God's heart for you: Would he make you wait in vain? Do you think he would make you wait only to be disappointed? I think not. God is a good Father with good intentions. The Bible in Isaiah 60:22 says, *"... I am the LORD; in its time I will do this swiftly"*. The whole of Isaiah chapter sixty is full of God's promises and blessings to his people. Promises that anyone would eagerly look forward to. In the last verse of the chapter, after God had stated all the promises, he proclaims his sovereignty and demonstrates that time is a crucial factor in ensuring the manifestation of the promises. The time within which the promises occur matters and when the time comes you won't have to ask, it will happen faster than the speed of light. I hope knowing this will give you the strength to let go of whatever or whomever you are desperately clinging to and instead trust in God's timing.

***

The thoughts I'll share in this section are some of the experiences that propelled me to write this book. I have been a part of a number of girl chats with various single ladies, talking about boys, relationships and our future goals and dreams. You would probably know that such conversations are fun and exciting until they are not. I came to embrace singleness from a Christian standpoint in my first year of college. I was reading books, watching sermons and learning from other Christian ladies and it was exciting for all of us, but as time went by, fear started to sneak in. As we grew older, friends and relatives began to make comments and ask questions, and eventually, the positive vibes turned into sad vibes. It seems the society expects women to be married by a certain age and as you approach that specific age you need to ensure that you have secured a boyfriend and you are heading towards that direction. Sadly most women believe it and put pressure on themselves to make it happen. I fell for it too and I started to think I had to try harder by "putting myself out there," you know how it goes. However, I realised that what society said and what I believed about myself did not match what God's Word said about me. And at that moment, I decided I would no longer believe that lie and instead I would press on and believe only God's Word. I love my family and friends, and I'm sure certain things that have been socially constructed have worked for most people. But as God's Child, I choose to do things his way and accept that it may differ from the social norm. In the kingdom of God, we don't entertain worry, we overcome fear and we remain more than conquerors by sticking to faith.

Ladies, there was a point I actually felt exhausted by conversations about dating, marriage, courtship, and relationships. We need to dispel the misconception that we are living for this moment only to get married one day. You are a Child of God, set apart for him, your life began the moment you made Christ your Lord and saviour. Decide that you won't be one of the sad girls. Having marriage aspirations does not mean you should spend your single years helpless and sad. Choose to live your life now as a single woman to the glory of God.

As for me, I set certain standards for myself to ensure I remain joyful, hopeful and present to my singleness. I am a work in progress and setting such measures requires constant accountability. However, I know my life has taken a turn for the better since I started following these principles.

OVERCOMING SAD VIBES

Sorrow usually occurs in moments when your hope wears thin because things do not seem to be going your way. As a single woman, you can say you are waiting on the Lord but you put a date on it. You attach certain conditions to your period of "waiting". Sometimes, you may be waiting on a "certain guy" and when he gets hitched your hearts sinks. Other times you may be "waiting" with a specific year in mind and when that year goes by, your hope goes with it. I don't say this to shame you ladies but you've got to do something about it.

Let's look at some of my suggested measures:

1) STICK IT OUT

As you proactively await marriage do not do things over excessively. You need to understand that I am not taking how you feel lightly. Instead, I am asking you to loosen up a bit. If things are not going the way that you anticipated do not let sorrow fill your heart. I know the first person we hold responsible for our life happenings is God. So, when something unlikely occurs we blame God for allowing it to happen and so we assign fault to him. We say things like:

- God didn't answer my prayer
- God probably doesn't want me to have this

We even go further and place blame on ourselves:

- I didn't pray enough
- I probably did something wrong

- I don't possess enough faith
- We even include the devil, by concluding that it is an attack from him

When something doesn't happen according to our preferred order we get frustrated and disoriented. Most people make the conclusion that "Something wrong must have happened". Instead of assigning blame, my suggestion to you is, if you cannot wrap your head around the, "why?" Don't hurt your head trying to figure it out. Accept that you had prayed and hoped for things to happen a certain way and they didn't and move forward guided by the assurance of God's faithfulness. So maybe you prayed that by thirty you would be married and that hasn't happened and you are wondering did God really hear my prayer. Yes, he did.

We don't always get the answer immediately or within our preferred timeframe. In other instances, you get a whole different outcome than the one you expected because sometimes, God's answer is, not healing but resurrection[4]. What you need to hold on to is this, God answers prayers. Embrace the time before the answer. Our God is a God of precision. Part of the process may include moulding you to graciously receive by removing your sense of entitlement. For a single woman, God may say, no, to a spouse right now and yes, to the renewing of your mind to resolve your initial desperation for marriage. Understand that it is all part of the process. Maybe reconciliation with your family is part of your answered prayer for a spouse. Just a thought. I am not stating these examples to suggest that you've asked amiss. This is just to say that there is a time for everything, and it is vital that you realise what season of life you are in. Know that, God loves you enough to allow you to go through certain paths before you get your answered prayer.

Also, talk to God about it. I've experienced this in my own life that sometimes, I am afraid to talk to God about the very thing I believe he is responsible for bringing about (or not bringing about). I mean who would want to make God look bad? Asking alone is like you are claiming that God doesn't answer prayer. I've truly found myself in a conundrum (many times, if I may add) when something, unlike my initial prayer request, happens. Some of you, have firmly been taught never to ask God, why. So, you keep quiet and suck it up as you hurt inside. It hurts when you don't receive from God the response that you initially wanted. No one should tell you not to cry about it. You can grieve while still possessing such great faith. Reacting with emotion does not express a lack of faith. Do not deny your feminine heart from expressing emotion. Steven Furtick wrote, "The presence of God is not a place to bypass emotions; it's a place to process them[5]." So after you have cried or even as you cry, stir yourself up in faith knowing that God's Word is final when he says, I hear and answer your prayers. He does just that. It doesn't mean God's power has somehow stopped functioning on your behalf. Having that knowledge in mind, go about your life assured and joyful that God will come through for you. If sadness tries to creep into your heart declare and remind yourself that the Lord will never fail you. Have fun with it by choosing to insanely trust in God even when you can't physically identify any progress towards the marriage you are awaiting. Out-persist the devil, the powers and principalities of this world and every anxious or worrisome thought by remaining steadfast on God's Word

2) BE PRESENT

There are so many things that call for your attention in the present day including making plans for your future. It is so easy to get caught up in planning for the future that you don't enjoy the present. You ought to embrace every moment you spend as a single woman. Every day won't always be rosy and not all days will be unbearable. You have to learn to take the good with the bad.

Ladies, you can enjoy being single while you are waiting. It is possible. We all have days when we would rather live with our heads in the clouds, imagining, but trust me you don't want to miss a thing. There is no insignificant day in your life; every day should be lived to the fullest. Don't allow any distractions to steal you away from today. I believe the only way you can live in the present is if you hold on to the assurance that God will take care of your future. Let God sort out your future.

It's beautiful when I imagine that God has already gone before me. For that reason, I don't need to jump ahead of myself. I don't know about you but I get excited when I think of the good future God has planned out for me. There are days that I get so excited, I could jump out of my skin. Imagining with God and looking ahead towards the future we hope for is part of the beautiful period of waiting. You will notice that when you are dreaming with God, there will be days that the future feels so close you could touch it. Yet, even when you are so engrossed in your hope for the future; you still need to have your feet planted in the present. Realise that, you are here, in the now and this is where you need to be. You are here for a good reason. You cannot get to tomorrow without getting through today. Waiting is part of the process. Trust the process.

There are things that only single women get to experience. Some could make your life miserable if you read too much into them especially since you would rather be coupled up. For example, how many of us, when asked have actually raised up our hands in church, to identify as singles? You would rather keep your hands down, right? The need to be in a relationship is cultivated when we are very young and as we get older the need grows stronger. It's easy to live with marriage on your brain. So absorbed in your possible future that you get so distracted from the present. But, what will you say of your single years? Life will gradually slip by while you are busy trying to attain something currently out of your reach. Recognise that God's got you. He is the God of your present. He is out to make your life right now, great! He has plans for you, single lady. Living your best life also applies to you, today. Accept that you are here in the now. Make the most of it. You will look back with no regrets if you are fully present in your singlehood. You will get the best of both worlds: Life as a single woman and as a wife! It all starts with your decision to live fully single today; embracing every moment. As you await marriage, don't get distracted and go searching for your man and let life pass you by.

3) STAY AWAY FROM YOUR GUILTY PLEASURES

We all have our go-to sources of comfort on the days when we feel emotionally low. It could be watching cutesy videos on YouTube or checking Instagram posts of the ideal couples you follow. Maybe you have a go-to rom-com? You are not doing anything unusual by indulging yourself in a little romantic daydreaming. There are days when you need that extra encouragement from observing others who have great relationships. I would actually encourage you to prayerfully consider identifying an ideal couple that you can look up to. It is important to learn from those who have gone before you. Maybe right now there are couples that you may admire including couples made up of individuals who are not grounded in Christ. When it comes to that sort of couple, you may not want to emulate everything about them. However, in as much as you would want to model only after Christian couples, you can't ignore the fact that whether unbelievers or believers certain couples hold valuable traits that would prove useful to anyone. The only thing needful is that you put under a microscopic lens of the Word of God everything you learn from either couple and purposefully surrender to God the aspects of other people's relationships that inspire you. I know for sure that God is an expert at making sense of our intricate feelings. When you surrender to God, he will shape your desires and align them with his.

Ok, let's get back on track. Where do you run to when you fill sad and lonely? What do you do on the days you feel a little extra sappy with thoughts of future *bae* on your mind? I have learnt that you have to do whatever it takes to remain a healthy single. Every woman gets emotional triggers from everywhere! You see a dad with his baby girl and you drift away in thoughts of the father-daughter relationship, your future spouse and daughter would have. You see a house and you think of your ideal family home. You see a pregnant woman and you imagine what it would be like if you were having a baby.

Clearly, thoughts are a doorway to daydreaming, whether you interact with visual or audio material; you are free to paint pictures of the future in your mind. Therefore, it is so important to keep yourself in check. You should know when you get obsessive over something and to always surrender whatever it may be to God. In this case, surrendering to God involves simply telling him how certain things make you feel, admitting the amount of time you spend on them and also acknowledging to God that it is your source of comfort. You probably know where I am going with this and what I will say next:

God should be your ultimate source of comfort. The Bible clearly says that the Holy Spirit is our comforter[6]. Whatever assurance you may need, you can receive it from the Holy Spirit. Instead of indulging in your "guilty pleasures," you can free your conscience by surrendering your feelings and inclinations to God as often as the need arises. You will experience more freedom, as you practice the art of surrender. You will no longer need to run to temporary fixes when overpowered with emotion. You will be able to stand.

There will be days when surges of emotion concerning your marital future will resurface. Instead, of seeking comfort in videos, audio, Instagram posts or blogs, find your solace in God. With help from the Holy Spirit, you will enjoy content on love and marriage without having any unhealthy attachment towards it.

4) MAKE PRAYER A PRIORITY

There is literally no other way to get through your singleness without prioritising the time you spend with God. There is no limit to the things that you can pray for. The beauty of prayer is that you talk directly to God and you can also spend time hearing from him.

You could get advice from friends, your pastor and multiple people about marriage. However beneficial those talks may be, they cannot compare to your personal quiet time with God. As a matter of fact, it would be better for you to spend more time in prayer than in discussions. God is an expert on love. In addition to that, he is also the one who is adequately equipped to teach you how to best enjoy singlehood. Like I said before, it is important that you get to enjoy the best of both worlds, as a single woman and as a married woman. So the reference to prayer here is for the prayers you will make for your future and also prayers for your current season.

Prayer will get you through your bad days and you can equally celebrate good days through prayer. You may be wondering how one can celebrate through prayer. Well, you can narrate to God your hopes and dreams. You could also talk to God about the strides you are making in your faith as an unmarried woman.

The Bible encourages us to pray continually because one way to hear from God is through prayer. There is absolutely no substitute for prayer. You've got to draw near to God in your singleness. Be intentional about hearing from him because even when you are not intentionally listening there will be loud messages on billboards, in songs, and various media instilling their opinions in you. You've got to have a clear focus on Jesus. Set your mind on him.

TRUE CONTENTMENT

True contentment is the outcome of fully yielding to God while navigating through the waiting process. By the grace of God, you will settle in and fully embrace your singleness. Singleness will no longer feel like a burden. When pressure arises you will possess the right tools to combat stress and comparison. You would have come to know that you are not disadvantaged because you are single and you won't feel the need to rush the waiting process. I know that in light of all your struggles right now, this may feel like an ambitious goal. As in, could one truly be content?

I promise you that it is the same principles laid out in this book that helped me stop chasing for contentment in relationships. A lot of unmarried women believe that all their problems will be solved once they get married. Sometimes we conclude that once we are married, we would have levelled up, society will accept us and that we have a shot at truly being happy. Darling, there is a better way that allows you to be content in every season. Paul shared in, Philippians 4: 12-13, that he discovered the secret of being content in any and every season: *"I have learnt the secret of being content in any and every situation, whether well fed or hungry, whether living in plenty or in want. I can do all things through him who gives me strength."* Therein lies the secret to being content. I found myself saying, "Lord, I want to stay here a bit longer." Don't let this little prayer scare you. For me, longer does not quantify to additional days, weeks, months or years of singlehood. What this means is that every woman should remain joyful, alive, fulfilled and confident for as long as she is single. Being content does not downplay your struggle, rather it changes the focus to God's empowering strength working in and through you. You are simply making a choice between obsessing over worry and focusing on God. Leave the days of feeling sorry for yourself behind. There is nothing wrong with you because you are single. You are not broken and incomplete.

You need to come to a place where you completely accept your singleness and fully embrace every aspect of it. It is much better than living your single years constantly wishing you were married. Always trying to get out. It is possible to be a genuinely happy single woman.

When you are discontent as a single woman, the desire to get married becomes larger than life. As you watch your peers get married and you feel the intense pressure to also marry. This is the most vulnerable time for any single woman. During that time, your predicament could either make you or break you. You could accept defeat and give up or you could persevere and come out the other side stronger and a better version of yourself. I believe that the best time to overcome a problem is during the moments when you feel the most pressed. Let your current stage in singleness make you better. True contentment can only be produced when you have been squeezed the most. This point in your journey won't make you only into a better wife. It will also make you, an all-around great person. The difficult times are key to developing you into a more mature Christian.

Dear beloved, I want you to enter into marriage having enjoyed your single years to the fullest. It is possible not to worry about your future. It is possible to fully live in the present while hoping for a beautiful marriage. It is also possible to intercede for your future from a place of contentment. Explore these possibilities, don't worry your way to marriage. You will know you are truly content when you are not constantly wanting to take on the role of your future self.

CHAPTER THREE

LOVE WILL FIND YOU

"Love is not something you go out and look for. Love finds you, and when it does, ready or not, it'll be the best thing to ever happen to you."
Anonymous

Single women put so much pressure on themselves to be the "perfect" woman for the ideal man they have in their minds or their current crush. They change themselves according to the liking of this "ideal man" to capture his attention. For example, if he likes rap music, the lady acquaints herself with hip-hop and if this fellow detests women who wear clothes that "show some skin", the lady resorts to wearing long-sleeved tops and maxi skirts. There is clearly a problem if you have to put on a façade with the sole purpose of finding love. The idea of making yourself, "loveable" to attract a potential spouse is deplorable. It's unfortunate that you would have to go to those lengths to present yourself as worthy. Yet, I fully understand why you would resort to those measures because singleness has been presented as a questionable relationship status, especially if you have reached a certain age.

I urge all of you ladies to stop trying to modify yourselves in order to please a "potential" suitor. You are worth so much and there is no reason for you to devalue yourself. You were perfectly made in Christ's image and you shouldn't doubt yourself. You are worth far more than rubies

(Proverbs 31:10). When God created you, he made a masterpiece (Ephesians 2:10). You are one of a kind. When your future husband meets you he will find a good thing. You are worthy of unconditional love. So can you and I agree that we will stop focusing so much on trying to earn someone's love and just love ourselves in the same way Christ has loved us?

When you meet the right person, you won't have to pretend to be someone else or force someone to fall in love with you. My desire for you is that you get to a place where you know your self-worth. A place where you don't see yourself as a "charity case," so desperate to find love. You are a priceless gem. God gave up the best of heaven, Jesus Christ to die for you. Why would you want to adjust yourself to attract someone who doesn't see your worth?

REBEKAH'S LOVE STORY

One of the love stories from the Bible that has become a personal favourite is the story of Rebekah and Isaac. The story is found in Genesis 24. At this time, Abraham had advanced in years and was nearing his death; for this reason, he wanted to find a suitable wife for his son Isaac. Abraham sent his servant, Eliezer to look for a wife for Isaac from his country of origin, Aram Nahariam. When he got to the country, Eliezer stopped by a well and prayed in his heart asking God to give him success that day. He specifically asked God for a sign that would indicate the woman as the one God had chosen for Isaac. The sign was that the woman would offer him a drink of water when he asked her for one and, that she would also offer to water his camels without him asking. Before he finished praying Rebekah showed up and she was carrying a jar on her shoulder. To cut the long story short, he got everything and more than what he had asked for in prayer. It was a perfect answered prayer.

LESSONS FROM REBEKAH

i. YOU ARE PERFECT FOR SOMEBODY

There is a man out there who is praying for a woman like you. You carry all the qualities and characteristics that he admires in a woman. You are perfect for him. Beloved child of God, you will not have to change anything about yourself to earn his love. There will definitely be things that you *will* have to change as a way of improving yourself so as to accommodate another human being. But you won't be compromising on your beliefs and principles. There exists someone who will have eyes only for you. So, maybe you are not like the other girls who you've seen get married. You probably do not carry yourself the way they do. You are that Christian girl that is a little "extra" compared to the others and sometimes you feel like, "who will be interested in me with all these strict standards." Does that sound like you? Great! Me too. In a world where it is so easy to compromise your standards, God's values still remain unchangeable and because you've chosen to do things God's way you will appear "strange". But God is still looking for women after his own heart who will redefine the concept of love that the world has become accustomed to. Women who will say, "We will do things God's way and still expect to find love"

ii. GO ABOUT YOUR BUSINESS

Keep doing what God has put right in front of you. **Everyone** has something that God has put right in front of them. It could be school, a job or everyday household tasks. If you are a student, keep doing your schoolwork, if you are employed, your job requires all the time and effort you can give to it right now. And if you are at home, do your chores, pick up that book you've been meaning to read, take longer showers, and spend time with your family. The bottom line is your life doesn't need to stop so that every drop of your energy is spent pondering and devising your future. Don't go out looking with your wandering eye trying to manipulate situations in order for them to work to your advantage. Let him find you!

For Rebekah, she went to draw water like any other day and she didn't know what God had in store for her on that specific day. At this time Rebekah was already eligible for marriage and yet she continued to do her regular duties. A proposal at the well? I have no doubt that she didn't see that coming. You know you have successfully trusted God when God has to interrupt you to give you the spouse you asked him for. You are not trying to earn it. As a result, when you meet him it will truly be a gift. You will be a witness of God's goodness and God will get all the glory for it.

iii. STAY HIDDEN

Rebekah wanted to get married. She didn't even hesitate to leave her family and go to a new land (Genesis 24: 57). Moreover, she had the option of not accompanying Eliezer even after she was showered with many lavish gifts from the family of her potential suitor (Genesis 24: 53) and yet she *chose* to go.

There was something beautiful that she did in Genesis 24: 64-65. When Rebekah arrived in the land where Isaac lived, she saw a man from afar and inquired of him. When she found out that that man was Isaac, Rebekah took her veil and covered herself. Now I find this interesting because even after she knew that this was the man who would be her husband, she didn't rush into making herself noticed but instead she hid herself until Isaac took her into his tent (Genesis 24: 67). She waited for Isaac to make the first move.

I've played this scenario a number of times before in my head but with a different twist. I would have expected Rebekah to get off her horse, remove her veil and approach Isaac confidently with a smile on her face announcing, "The woman of the house is here." You would think that knowing that Isaac was the man she would marry automatically gave Rebekah the right to run forth towards Isaac and meet him, but she did no such thing. Instead, she left Abraham's trusted servant to do all the necessary talking. She knew that there was a procedure to be followed.

I believe Rebekah knew that even though Eliezer had brought her to Canaan to be Isaac's wife, the union would only be official if Isaac personally took her in as his wife. And as history narrates, the union only became official when Isaac was on the same page as everyone else and personally decided he would marry Rebekah (Genesis 24:67).

There are women who believe, God has shown them their future husband— I personally don't believe that is impossible. God can do anything. However, I do believe it should be approached with caution. There was evidence of God's overt involvement in the events that occurred surrounding Rebekah as narrated by Eliezer (Genesis 24:34- 50; Genesis 24:66) that all the parties involved seemed to agree with. There was a mutual understanding that existed among all involved parties that happened without any imposition. If, you believe God has shown you your future husband, let it play out without your involvement. If God can communicate with you, he can also communicate with the other person. So, until God also reveals to your future husband that you are meant to be together don't unveil yourself, stay hidden.

Or maybe you might have a crush on a certain fellow and you feel all the stars have aligned. This is "the one." You truly know it in your heart. Proving what others have said, "When you know, you know." Maybe you are extremely impatient and you are convinced you just have to let this guy know how you feel. Child of God, it's is not your place. I believe just as Rebekah had Eliezer; today, we also have a mediator, Jesus Christ. Through the Holy Spirit, he speaks individually to our hearts. He knows how to correctly articulate feelings and unite two people who are destined to be together.

Another way, I believe you can stay hidden as a woman in this modern day is if you don't take on wife responsibilities before you are declared a wife. Yes, you may be engaged and you know you will get married one day. But until your union is blessed at church and agreed upon by your parents, remain hidden— not only concerning purity. I think women in relationships sometimes get too comfortable. For instance, by going to their partner's house to wash his clothes on weekends and performing other chores, just literally taking over his household. There are other things that one would do as a girlfriend that are understandable like attending weddings and funerals in his family but only as a guest, nothing more. You remain a visitor until you are made a wife.

I have a friend who even while she was engaged and only a few months away from her wedding day, still upheld her principles. She never went to the guy's house if he was alone and if they were in a car they talked in open spaces with the windows down. Just in case you thought I was exaggerating; you cannot be too hidden.

A TIME SUCH AS THIS

Whether deliberately or without realising it, there are single women who are shaping their lives around their future spouse. In turn, this is keeping these women from undertaking their present responsibilities. Before you throw stones at me consider some of the things you say:

- Why should I dress up as if I have a boyfriend?
- I am saving the trip to Hawaii for my honeymoon.
- I will pursue my Master's degree after I get married.
- I will read the Song of Songs when I am married.
- When I get married, my husband will help me take care of my family.
- I cannot take a job in a remote area because no men will see me there.
- When I get married, I'll buy a house like that.

How many times has your future spouse or your prospective marriage governed your life's choices? On the outlook, it may appear cute since by faith you are planning for a life together with the future partner that you are trusting God for. However, it is to an extent dangerous. You are only playing it safe to keep from doing what God has called you to do in your current season.

I want you to pause for a minute and consider what you should be doing right now but instead have put aside as a future undertaking. Some of the examples listed above would make sense if God had specifically instructed you to do so. Then it would be cute and romantic. But how many of you have actually come up with those restrictions all on your own when you know you could actually carry out these goals during the period of your singleness? Is the idea of being single and alone stopping you from accomplishing these goals? Are you failing to visit certain countries, interact with some charities because you are single? If you honestly observe your actions and words you will discover that, to a certain degree, you have replaced God's roles and responsibilities with the spouse you wish for. Let's stop for a second, reflect and repent:

All-forgiving Dad, forgive me for placing my future spouse above you. Today, I begin to place more priority in the life I have in Christ. I can and I will do what you have called me to do today. I will by your grace start the much-needed workout and diet. I will go back to school because you are my provision. (Continue to insert whatever you've been putting aside). In Jesus' name. Amen

My girl, God is all you need. Look at Ruth in the Bible, a woman who was daring in her faith. A widow with no man to provide for her during a time when a woman's identity was assigned by her attachment to a man (either brother, father or husband). The Bible records that Ruth went out one day to work in the fields expecting favour from whichever harvester would allow her to pick leftovers from the yield. It was unusual for a woman to be the breadwinner in her family but because of their predicament, Ruth took on the responsibility of providing for herself and her mother-in-law, Naomi, who was also a widow.

Ladies, we always talk about finding our Boaz. But do you see Ruth's life's priorities and faith before she met Boaz? She trusted God. The only other solution for a widow at this time as eluded to by Naomi was to remarry (see Ruth 1: 11-13). Their way out of poverty would be to find other husbands. Their future success completely relied on marriage. As a widow, Ruth could have chosen to wallow in self-pity. So, Ruth setting out to work in a foreign country and going forth expecting favour was really a bold move. Just as God responds to every move of faith, he made a way for her.

By the time Ruth met Boaz she had already established that God was the supplier of her needs. May God, be all that you need. May, you know him as the supplier of your needs, your healer, your best friend, and your happiness. The Lord says, "I am yours and you are mine[1]". Let your satisfaction be in him alone. Set the foundation for your future marriage by making God the centre of your life, today. Let your life be driven by who God is and be motivated by what he is capable of doing through you.

I admire you if you are pursuing what God has placed in your heart at such a time as this. Don't be afraid to take on certain roles and responsibilities because you are single. Because of Jesus, you are single and capable. It should not be unusual for a woman who is single to pursue what God has purposed in her heart. It will not make you miss your Boaz. As a matter of fact, you will meet your Boaz along the way in pursuit of your God purposed dreams and accomplishments.

PRACTICAL PRINCIPLES

There are practical principles that you should live by as a single woman to ensure you remain disciplined in the wait. These suggestions will keep you out of trouble and will leave you feeling pleased with yourself and grateful that you used them. There are moments when you will be required to work out what you claim to believe. It's not always easy but by the grace of God, it's possible.

This involves actively pursuing what you believe. Joseph had to flee when Potiphar's wife tried to seduce him (Genesis 39: 6- 12). Esther, although she was favoured by the king's eunuch, Hegai, was still expected to go through the mandatory yearlong beautifying process (Esther 2: 12). In the same way, as a single woman, you have to be intentional about the things you do knowing full well that your actions corroborate your faith. The principles below have been developed over a lifetime, it's a result of a series of decisions, nothing happened within a day. As you go through these principles don't feel pressured to restrict yourself to these alone. They might appear as stringent measures but I promise you they will save you from a lot of trouble.

1. THE POWER TO SAY, NO

In this lifetime, you will have to say a couple of noes before you give your best yes. In certain circumstances, it will require all of your strength to let go of something or someone. The little word, no has the power to direct your life.

Sometimes turning down a certain guy's advances is no brainier; you know immediately that you and he would never work out so you don't even give it a chance. But there are other times when it's not easy to reject a guy. For instance, you may not want to be in a romantic relationship with him but you like the attention he is giving you and so it becomes difficult to stay away. You become hesitant to say, no.

Experience forces me to say this ladies, not every Christian guy that asks you out is the "one". Just because you have things in common with a certain man and he possesses the ideal qualities you've marked out of your future spouse does not make him the right one for you. There will be men who seem perfect. The kind who meets most of the qualities on your "checklist". But sometimes even, if you have feelings for him, there could be something off that maybe only you would know. Not that anything is wrong with him but you are just not compatible. You would know if he doesn't quite fit as the companion with whom you would want to spend the rest of your life. It could be that you don't completely agree on certain beliefs. It doesn't even have to be spiritual, it could be differences in how you handle finances. It also includes, how you relate at an emotional level.

I know you may think, "But men will label me as difficult and won't approach me." Unfortunately, some women forfeit their right to be particular about the partner of their choice believing that they're not a lot of men who would be interested in them. In your search to find a good man, God is faithful. Raise your faith and trust God for a spouse and refuse to let fear dictate your choices. Take captive to the obedience of Jesus Christ the thought that you will have to scramble to find yourself a good man or any man at all.

Sweetheart, God always makes good on his promises. The Bible says about Sarah, *"She considered him faithful who had made the promise"* (Hebrews 11: 11). God worked wonders before for Sarah when she couldn't conceive a child, he is still the same God today. Trust him. You will certainly be approached by guys who are truly sincere and not in any way short of excellence but not the suitable companion God has for you. Ladies, I am asking you to pass up good for great. If you are not a hundred percent sure about a guy do not get involved with him. I am asking you not to settle for anyone less than God's best. When it concerns love and a lifetime commitment, almost doesn't count. When you know, "he could be but he's not," be brave enough to walk away.

It will surely take courage for you to let go of a "solid opportunity". So, remember God won't leave you alone, he will give you the grace to walk away. God knows we throw tantrums when our ideal request is delayed or altered. Yet, God is so gracious and patient with us. He is also kind and protective of us. I once prayed for God to make a specific guy "notice me." Within the same week, this guy that I had never spoken to in my life, approached me and showed interest in me. You can imagine my excitement when I got my "answered prayer." Needless to say, it didn't turn out quite as I expected—let's just say I wasn't the only girl he was pursuing. Ladies, I dodged a bullet with that one. But it didn't feel that way because even though that was the case I still wanted him to choose me. I remember he was blunt about what he wanted from me (it was not in any way pure). I turned him down knowing that I wouldn't be conducting myself in a Christ honouring manner. For another believer, the outcome of this scenario may seem inevitable but when feelings are involved, our values get tested and certain boundaries become blurred.

It is also possible that my story may sound frivolous to some of you because you may have found yourself in more intense situations, but I just want to show you that God is always there for you and he will be there when you need to give that decisive, no. God is so good that he will protect us from even our own senseless desires by empowering us to walk away. His grace is sufficient for us. Ladies, until you receive a solid, go-ahead from God, let your answer remain, no.

2. GUARD YOUR HEART (LICENSE TO BE RUDE?)

"Above all else guard your heart for it is the well spring of life" (Proverbs 4:23). "Guard your heart," is a general statement made to caution you about being aware of the things that occupy your heart. Whatever you allow to fester in your heart will direct your life. However guarding your heart does not mean, being uptight, pushing people away, or being cold. It was common throughout my school days— from the time I was in primary till college, for a girl to reject a guy's advances by telling them off in the most disrespectful and embarrassing ways you could imagine. I personally found it to be problematic.

It is not unusual for men to approach a woman they find attractive. If that was non-existent, your mum and dad would probably not be together. Men are God's creation and he is the one who has blessed them with the spirit of courage and persistence. Does it get unbearable sometimes? Definitely! One thing that stands out for every girl is, receiving unwanted attention from guys. It's dreadful. The catcalling, the stares and worse still, when these types of guys decide to approach you. In those scenarios, most girls are thinking, "I didn't ask for this." You could be wearing the longest maxi skirt ever made and somehow you still attract their attention. I am yet to meet an emotional and irritated lady who has only ever acted civil towards such men. I know I've acted defensively, especially because I blamed myself for attracting such attention. Many are the times when the majority of the guys who are "bold" in approaching you don't behave decently and you deduce that their terrible actions reflect back to you. As in: "If this type of guy is hitting on me, I did something wrong and brought it on myself." Darling, guard your hearts against this erroneous belief that you are the problem. If a guy is a pervert or scornful towards you, he is clearly the one who's in the wrong, not you. So, don't throw disheartening labels at yourself.

I believe you can be assertive in showing disinterest to such irrational men without stooping down to their level. I know it gets annoying, the perusing and whistling are uncalled for and uncomfortable. You may feel justified to throw insults at such men because they've hurt your feelings. But, you are not of this world, you are not like the other girls who act that way. God will fight for you even in such scenarios. I don't know about you but it matters that God fights for me in such circumstances because I consider these men's behaviour towards me to be offensive and belittling which sometimes leaves me hurt and having self-doubt. As you obey the beautiful command to guard your hearts make sure that you don't get carried away with over-protectiveness that you lose the guard over your mouth.

3. STAY IN YOUR LANE

You can't be single but also "available"— as in women who are present and linger around men but claim to be single. They flirt and flaunt their looks giving men the green lights but as soon as a man approaches and shows interest in them, their attitude becomes hostile. Sometimes, the lady goes even further to receive all the benefits that would have come if she was in a relationship with the man but turns him down when he states his intentions of making their relationship official.

You are without a doubt exceptional and men will be interested in you but don't lead them on. You can't say, "I am single and waiting on God" when you are covered in green neon lights signifying otherwise. You have to walk the talk. Your conduct has to match what you are saying. Don't ever behave in such a way that you could be mistaken for the other women who are "available". Other people's testimony of you should be an assurance that you are truly disciplined and not trying to evoke attention from men.

If you spend long hours on the phone with this guy, sharing your dreams and goals, without a doubt you will become emotionally attached to each other. I know it's not easy because you are genuinely being a good friend sometimes. However, if there is a possibility that it will get too far you just have to cut loose any ties with that male friend or make your stance clear between the two of you. You may think these measures are a bit too extreme but think about it, you want to settle down with the next man you date. So if you know that you are becoming entangled with a man with whom you will not spend the rest of your life, why should you then invest your emotions and time on him?

I strongly advise that your "Waiting on the Lord" should not involve leading guys along and eventually tossing them away. You have to be clear from the get-go. Ladies, you know when you are stringing a guy along. If you know that it will not lead into a well-formed relationship, leave it, it's not for you. That man has another lady waiting for him, our sister somewhere is praying for this man. It is wrong for you to treat him like your boy toy. Let him go! God will bring someone your way and if you are lonely and bored, allow God to fill your void and occupy your time, he promises a more abundant life (John 10:10).

4. DON'T FALL FOR JERKS

According to the Merriam-Webster dictionary, a jerk is someone who is rude, small-minded, and cruel.[2] Some men are downright nasty and disrespectful towards women. Their form of pursuit is to be mean and aggressive towards a woman in an attempt to win her over. Ladies, don't even give these men a second of your time. The first sign of crudeness is your cue to leave! They say things like, "You want to get married right? Then why are you playing hard to get?" Toss that boy into the friend zone or don't be his friend at all. I've heard men say, *"Atsikana enanu mumangovuta koma sikuti ndiinu okongola"*[1] . Why would you want to be with that kind of man? His motto is probably, "Devalue her till I can get her" He is not worth your time! Yes, you want to get married but do not trade in your hard-earned principles in order to please mediocre men.

Ladies, when did you become "humble?" Why would you allow for men to degrade you? Do you doubt how precious you are? The world has portrayed having "self-worth" as being proud and full of yourself. So, now as women, we shy away from being self-confident for fear that we will appear arrogant.

For instance, a virgin in the Bible is an exceptional description of an unmarried woman. However, staying a virgin until marriage has been degraded in this contemporary world and categorised as uncool and primitive. It's depicted as something one ought to be ashamed of. Like a certain man of God would put it, "That is a lie from the pit of hell!" If God is not ashamed of virgins, why are you ashamed of yourself? This does not mean you have to go out and announce your virginity to the whole world or look down on other women that are not virgins, but rather, you should own it. Never let anyone make you feel worthless and less beautiful for being a virgin or unmarried.

I know men (and other women) say ridiculous things like "you won't be prepared for marriage (practice makes perfect)" and some tease you saying, you lack opportunity. Ladies, I know it hurts and you strongly want to defend yourself and maybe even at times, you've argued with your accusers. However, I want you to know that God is your defender, he will fight for you (Exodus 14:14). Don't waste your breath trying to explain profound matters to trivial people. All you have to do is obey what the Lord has said.

Walking in purity is only one area in which women are attacked but there are many areas and a number of ways that petty men dishonour women. Remember however, that there can only be one truth, you are

---

[1] *Some of you women are not even beautiful but you play hard to get*

worthy in God's sight. That's the first and final word over your life today and forever. Child of God, you can only fall for a jerk if you don't know the value God has placed on you. Know your worth. The truth is you never lose value in God's sight. Your age, disabilities, your history, your accomplishments or the lack thereof, do not weigh you down on God's scale. Remember you were to die for; a life was given for yours, and no price tag can be put on that.

5. DO NOT AWAKEN LOVE BEFORE IT'S TIME

There are four words for love, in Hebrew. Every word describes a different type of love. One particular word for love in Hebrew is, *Eros* and the English word, *Erotic* is derived from this Hebrew word. You may be familiar with the word English word, erotic which means to give in to sexual pleasures.[3] It is, therefore, obvious that this type of love is in its sense, sexual. The Word of God commands us saying, *"Do not lust"* (Matthew 5:28) and even further the Bible counsels against any type of extramarital sexual affairs (1 Corinthians 7:1-2). Therefore, if you are not married and are involved in erotic activities, you are awakening love before its time.

If you are a woman who has been sexually active prior to becoming celibate or you were exposed to lustful behaviour in any way, God is faithful to restore your mind and body. By the grace of God, you can gain self-control and live a life overcoming sexual sin. Also, be intentional about staying away from any sexual content including movies heavy laden with sexual references. The devil is stealing the joy of sex as intended by God to be between husband and wife by making common that which is sacred. I pray that God renews your lifestyle by restoring his will and esteem for sex in your heart. And as you pray for yourself tell God, *"Lord, I awakened love before it's time, restore my sanctity. "*It's never too late to choose God's way, in fact, that is actually more honouring to God. It is written, *"Obedience is better than sacrifice"* (1 Samuel 15:22). The Lord greatly values obedience and he is willing to work together with you and to place you on the path of righteousness. The Bible also says, *"Come now, let us reason together, says the LORD. Though your sins are as scarlet, they shall be as white as snow; though they are red as crimson, they* *shall be like wool"* (Isaiah 1:18). Only God knows how to make you live a life above sin, let him help you.

CHRIST PURSUES US

One of the qualities of love is that it pursues. God stripped himself of his glory, took on flesh and dwelt among us (John 1:14). He followed us to where we were: heaven came to us. It is because of this pursuit, we are now partakers of a goodly heritage in Christ Jesus. He gave us the greatest gift of all.

Have you ever had a secret admirer? A guy who sent you roses and gifts or sent his friends to talk to you? It's honestly a good feeling when you know there is someone out there who is interested in you and is studying you to find ways to get your attention.

In the same way, the Lord is pursuing us with his love. Take time to notice the sunshine and roses he is sending your way. God doesn't stop at your salvation and say, "Ok, I got her now I can stop pursuing her." He is still showering you with love and drawing you closer to himself. When you realise that Christ is pursuing you by virtue of being yourself, it's going to be easier for you to embrace who you are and the love Christ has for you.

Christ does not disqualify you by your attitude or flaws. He is not going to give up on you when you fail. There are a lot of times when we disqualify ourselves because of our failures. For example, saying, "No one will want to marry me with the nature of my past." God is pursuing you as you are and is transforming you into his likeness. You may not currently be the woman you aspire to be but that is not reason enough to expect the worst in your future. You place an unfair expectation on yourself if you are determined to have all the perfect qualities of a "proverbs 31 woman" by the time you get married. You will become the ideal woman and wife you want to be one day but cut yourself some slack and understand that you are a work in progress.

Christ's perpetual pursuit of us sets a standard of what we should expect from our future husband. It is written in Ephesians 5:25, *"Husbands love your wives like Christ loved the church..."* If you don't know how much Christ loved the church (you), how are you going to know what kind of love to expect from your future husband? Don't get me wrong, I know he won't be exactly like Jesus. Although, I do believe that your future husband's love towards you should be an extension of God's love.

Additionally, if a guy likes you, he should pursue you. Moreover, a guy who is serious about you will not be afraid to embark on the chase. He will make time for you and make you feel special. In his pursuit of you, this man should make you draw closer to the Lord, and not distract you from cultivating your relationship with God. A good man will take you as you are and understand that you are still growing and gradually become perfected in Christ.

GOD IS CLOSE TO THE BROKEN HEARTED

Your heart can turn sour if you have had a bad experience loving someone and it didn't turn out as you expected. My heart goes out to you if you have had to endure heartbreak as a result of a relationship. It does not matter when you experienced this heartbreak, whether in high school or in college. It may have been a long time ago or recently. Your heartbreak is still acknowledged by God.

Heartbreak is a sorrowful period in our lives that requires us to grieve and to heal. Heartbreak should not be taken lightly. God does not underrate a broken heart. The Bible says, *"God is close to the brokenhearted."*[4] God knows the heart is precious and for that reason charges us to watch over it above all else (Proverbs 4:23). When your tender heart has been crushed over and over again especially by those who were supposed to love you, it becomes hardened. So, maybe you opened your heart to love and in the end, you were left shattered. And now that you want to love again, your heart just won't let you. You are too afraid that you might get hurt again.

A broken heart leads to a distorted perspective that governs your actions. You need healing for your broken heart in order to properly love again. There is healing for you. I like the story that is told of Jesus that he literally died of a broken heart. His heart ruptured inside of him, he was hurt by the rejection he faced from man and also from his Father when he hang on the cross because of our sin. He also died inside in the same way you and I do when our hearts have been broken by the ones whom we love. He also just couldn't take it. He hurt. But the beauty is that he hurt so that you and I would be healed of our broken hearts. There is no wound too deep God cannot heal. No scar too exposed he cannot erase. No story too raw he cannot resolve. No memory too vivid he cannot make you forget. No sin so harmful, he cannot help you forgive. He will empower you to forgive and you will not hurt anymore.

Dear Father,

Restore all the broken pieces. Help me love again. Open my eyes to see true love and not to turn away from it. Give my feet strength to run towards love. Your perfect love. I forgive him {insert name}. I forgive him. I forgive them. My heart will not falter when I recall the hurt. I leave it all behind. I press forward to new beginnings. In Jesus's Name. Amen

TRUST GOD FOR YOUR PREPARATION

As you prepare for your future, it is important that you know God will equip you with the right tools to have a successful marriage. Everything does not depend on you! God has not left it up to you to sort out your life. Your success is on his mind and by his leading, you will have all the appropriate knowledge.

I have interacted with unmarried women who feel the pressure to become wife material. They acquire books, watch videos and get advice on marriage to ensure that they have adequate knowledge that will prepare them to be great wives. Don't get me wrong; it is admirable to be intentional and seek out information as someone aspiring for marriage. However, it is of grave importance that you don't get entangled in an obsessive pursuit of information that will compromise your morality.

I once cautioned a friend on who she allowed to teach her about marriage after she went to the extent of watching movies with adult content to learn about sex. I hope you get my point here, don't become extreme in your pursuit of a clear cut vision. Be led by the Spirit. You can only know so much now as an unmarried woman and you need to accept that certain knowledge is only appropriate for a woman as she draws closer to her wedding day. I also believe that other marital affairs can only be fully discovered within a marriage. Trust God for your preparation.

Consider a young girl competing for Miss Universe, against the world's most beautiful girls. Having no prior experience and only trusting what was handed to her. A young Hebrew girl named, Esther, found herself in a similar situation. An orphan raised by her uncle, Esther, was among the most beautiful virgin girls selected to be part of a pageantry, to find the next queen of Babylon, a country that stretched between 127 provinces.[5] She didn't know what to expect when she was taken to the palace for the yearlong mandatory preparation before meeting the king. But God caused Esther to find favour with Hegai, the king's eunuch who was in charge of all the girls and he offered her only the best care. When her turn came to meet the king, Esther found favour with the king, becoming Queen of Babylon.

The beauty of Esther's story is God was working behind the scenes the entire time. Although it was done covertly, God was in control, ordering all the pieces to work in Esther's favour. In the same way, you child of God are highly favoured[6], so you don't need to stress about how you are going to meet your "king". God's got you. He will put you in the right place at the right time and he will teach you all that you need to know in your preparation. The Bible says the anointing will teach you **all** things (John 16:12). The Word of God will cater to all your needs. Don't worry yourself sick with all the many emerging concerns. Only stick to the Word.

With everything I've said thus far, one may wonder, won't I become too complacent with my singleness, if I am so cautious? I felt that way once and I am not the only one. A guest writer shares her experience on the same in the next section and I truly believe you will be blessed by her account. In her own words, Elita writes:

TRUSTING GOD: AM I TOO CONTENT?

Do not be conformed to the behavior and customs of this world, but let God transform you into a new person by changing the way that you think. Then you will learn to know <u>God's will</u> for you which is <u>good</u>, and pleasing and perfect. – Romans 12:2

In the verse quoted above, I underline "God's will" and "good" because isn't that our question? Isn't that what we are sceptical about when it comes to romance or singlehood (or any facet of our life for that matter)? Can it be both "God's will" and yet simultaneously "good"? I will be the first to admit that I have, on many occasions, reasoned that my way was a lot more promising of a good end than God's way. I think that maybe this marred reasoning comes in because sometimes what God may be leading us to do, appears to make little sense to us. I mean just think about it; if I trust God enough to the point that I embrace this season of my singlehood, won't that make me too content and won't it keep me from putting myself out there? And if I don't put myself out there, how will I ever find my man? And if my man doesn't find me (or if we don't find each other), won't that leave me single till I'm 99 years old? Hahaha! As you know a girl's mind can be quite a rabbit hole as it is; we can map out a hundred possible outcomes from just one single thought, and I am no exception.

Seriously though, I may not be a 99-year-old lady right now, but, to be honest, I didn't really ever imagine myself to still be single today at 26 years old either. When I surrendered the pen of my love story to God way back in my college days (I think I was 21 years old at the time) God walked me through a season of teaching me about living a set-apart life. And as some of you might know, being set-apart and single in college is a fairly peculiar stance, and if you're single you can easily stand out as being rather odd. However, by the time I had gotten into the final year, it didn't even bother me so much that I was still single because by this time I was living rested in the truth that God is in control of my love life (non-existent as it was. Lol!). And this at-rest posture continued in me all the way into my post-grad years as well.

It doesn't really feel like an awkward weird thing to still be single anymore – I feel content! In fact (dare I say) I am enjoying being single! Believe it or not, being contentedly single has been a really nice experience for me – in fact, it's so nice of an experience that I started to get a little suspicious about myself. For example, I don't really have a lot of guy friends like I used to back then; and it has been ages since I was consistently engaging with any guy – I literally don't remember the last time I had a guy in my life (platonic or otherwise) who I text and talk with every single day. And the few guys that I do hang out with or who have shown any interest, have unceremoniously settled into the friend-zone.

So, what do we have here; is this a situation where my contentedness has just unknowingly banished me into a lifetime of singlehood? (And what you might find interesting to know is that even that thought doesn't freak me out – yes, you heard me right, I am content to be single, not only for now but even for the long haul). Don't get me wrong, I am not saying that I don't desire marriage; I do, and I look forward to meeting an amazing man one day. But I also recognize that an amazing man doesn't complete me; I am already complete; whether single or taken, Jesus is the one who completes me!

So what about my state of contentment? Have I gone too far; living too comfortable? Am I keeping myself too hidden or being too relaxed?

When I reach a stage where I feel that my contentment is problematic (cause sometimes I do worry that it might be) I choose to bring these issues to the Lord. I allow the Holy Spirit to perform heart surgery in me, like Rom 12:2 says, renew my mind. I might be content in my singleness and complete in Christ, but as a Christian, I am still in process. God exposes any fears and lies within me that might be holding me back, such as the fear of letting people in, or boundary issues, commitment problems, or even the lie that I might have banished myself to life-long singlehood – I bring all these things under the surgical blade of the Word of God. I have seen His truth expose the lies. Experiencing this has freed me from the worry that embracing singleness might be keeping me from meeting my future husband. One of the Bible stories about someone who was hidden is in 1 Samuel 16 – David was a shepherd boy, contentedly tending to his sheep folk in the unseen. He didn't put himself out there, actually one would almost think that he had banished himself from any hope of so much as a social life. But God is very capable and creative at fetching people out even from a hidden place. David was sought after from sheep duty to be anointed as king of Israel. David wasn't looking, yet God located him. Is God not capable of locating me too? He is able.

CHAPTER FOUR

SWORD OF THE SPIRIT—THE WEAPON AGAINST ANXIETY

"Cast all your anxiety on Him because he cares for you."

1 Peter 5:7

Anxiety presents itself in many forms through our fears, burdens, worries, and frustrations. We all get anxious. Sometimes in life, it only makes sense to worry over certain issues. It would actually be considered unusual if you didn't display any sign of anxiety over a difficult matter. Anxious thoughts disguise themselves as undeniable truths and they are not easy to spot. They fill your mind as your own opinions with great conviction. The Bible in the book of Philippians 4:6, says, *"Do not be anxious about anything but in everything by prayer and petition, with thanksgiving, present your request to God."* Worrying thoughts will always linger demanding your full attention but you can respond by remaining unmoved by placing your confidence in the Word of God which identifies and kills anxiety. In this chapter, I will show you how to use the Scriptures to identify and combat anxiety.

There are a lot of women who are struggling with being single. I believe the biggest anxiety among women who believe they are ready to be married is that if they don't find love in their prime age, their chances of getting married in the future will be limited. This anxiety spirals into other fears which leads one to question their worth and the outcome of their future.

It is enough cause for concern when you are not completely sure if a certain situation will turn out in your favour. However, that doesn't have to be your attitude, Child of God. Christ is your Anchor. You have a solid assurance for everything that you are believing for and his name is Jesus Christ, the Word of God. You don't have to live as a single woman, ever-anxious. You can look forward to a bright future because you have a sure hope.

DEALING WITH SHAME AND GUILT

We've all met some form of shame and guilt associated with love and relationships. Many people can relate to the awkwardness that existed between grown-ups and young people while growing up. Even the hypothetical, "when I get married" talk was met with a suspicious glare or sharp response. I came to learn that most of the older people suspected that if any young person made reference to marriage they were probably in a relationship with a member of the opposite sex. Yet that wasn't always the case. Every woman dreams of meeting Mr. Right and getting married. Therefore, it's not unusual to find young girls, teenagers, and even young adults constantly discussing love and marriage. For many, the reactions from the well-meaning elders incited shame and guilt towards having marriage aspirations. I personally fell into that guilt trap and I began to suppress any concerns, questions even the hopes and dreams I had with regards marriage. You would probably agree with me that even under all that suppression there remains a faint esteem for marriage that nudges at you to believe for something beautiful.

As a woman in this generation, expressing your aspirations for marriage is also met with contempt. A woman's aspirations to be married are seen as an admission that she can't sufficiently function as an individual. There exists a need to defend your decision and give people a good reason. So most women are compelled to conceal their dreams. It is fascinating that people will shame you for having marriage aspirations and they will also attack you for being single.

Women of faith probably meet the most persecution for desiring good and godly marriages. Once you are born into the family of God you discover a whole new meaning to love and marriage. You begin to learn *who* love is and you rediscover marriage according to God's initial design. Love from a godly perspective is better than any magical story you've been told about finding your knight in shining armour. God intended marriage to be a beautiful union between husband and wife. He set off the desire for marriage within our hearts even before we were born. However, those beliefs are met with another form of shame and guilt that comes with believing in healthy and wholesome relationships. You will meet a lot of resistance from well-meaning people for following your faith and seeking out a godly relationship marked by; faithfulness, purity, unreserved trust in Jesus and patience. A lot of believers who are on a similar path will tell you that doing things God's way is not very popular; it is rather ambitious. It would actually be easier and less cumbersome to jump on the bandwagon and be like everybody else.

The build-up of shame and guilt collected from all these different experiences easily suffocates hope. This is where the process of mind renewal comes into effect, to help you overcome such shame and guilt. It is a transformative journey of unlearning and unravelling that which you believed to be true, outside of God. As a believer, becoming grounded in your new-found godly beliefs as pertaining to marriage goes against a lot of what you've inherited from any long-standing family practices and popular culture. There is such deep-rooted shame and reproach coloured in culture and experience which silences the message of God's beautiful design for marriage. It's so important that you gain clarity of who you are and what you want and stick to it. If marriage represents to you, love and respect; simply make up your mind that you will cancel out all the negativity and pursue whatever is godly. Following in the footsteps of Joshua in Joshua 24:15, *"as for me and my house we will serve the Lord,"* resolve that you will believe and live by the love and marriage God has displayed in his Word. What are some attitudes you aspiring towards? Below are some thoughts:

- No fear of disappointment for completely trusting God with my love life
- I want my actions to reflect what I believe about a godly marriage

- I want a good marriage to be more real than all the bad I've seen
- I don't want to yield to the constant fear that even if I marry there is a chance that I could become a widow
- I want to come to terms with the notion that good men exist
- I want to stop rejecting the truth that a good marriage is possible for me
- I want to stop rejecting the truth that I will remain loveable to my husband as the years in our marriage advance.
- I want to stop accepting the lie that it is inevitable that my husband will cheat on me.
- I don't want to feel unworthy when I imagine my ideal man pursuing me.
- I don't want fear and doubt to dictate whom I date
- I don't want to stress over meeting my husband

Don't let shame and guilt fester. Tell God your hidden thoughts. It's so important to let out the thoughts and emotions that are bothering you. Stop carrying around the burden of shame for the aspirations you have. Release the thoughts that are causing you discomfort. The things that you are aspiring towards could be good and godly but the world wants to drag you down with it by suffocating your hope and so it becomes a struggle to believe. But you've got to fight every day to possess a sound mind. It won't be easy; it for sure requires discipline. Take heart in the fact that the hardest part is accomplished once you articulate your fears and hopes to God. Now you can begin to allow God to release his perfect love over your deepest concerns. This is what it means to surrender. Bring it all from the back of your mind and lay it all in its extremity before God. Overcoming shame and guilt places you in a better position to freely embrace your God-given hopes and dreams for marriage.

UNASHAMED TO ASK

I believe, when something keeps arising in your heart it's a deep conviction that God wants you to ask him for or about it. God promised us a new heart replacing our heart of stone (Ezekiel 36:26). On this new heart, God declared that he would write his new covenant, in order to reconcile us to himself (Hebrews 8:10). We would individually know him through his anointing. You have to realise that God is working in your heart (Phil 2:13). Therefore, don't condemn your own heart desires. Bring it up with God no matter how extreme it seems. Sometimes, you may scorn and laugh at yourself for desiring a good thing; putting it off as wishful thinking. I would encourage you to share your heart desires with God. He is waiting for you to talk to him about your desires.

You should be so comfortable with your desire that you can honestly and boldly articulate your hopes and beliefs about marriage whether it be among company or even to yourself.

I have noticed that people find it very uncomfortable to ask God for a spouse. They feel embarrassed because they assume meeting your companion should come "naturally." Well, while some do meet their spouses without much thought or prayer over it; others pray about it. This is because everyone's faith journey is different. In the same way, some would pray to conceive a child, for financial breakthrough or for healing. Certain individuals may not consider the above-mentioned examples as a problem so they don't invest their faith or offer much prayer on those concerns. However, for you, it may require faith and an investment in prayer for a spouse.

Do not fall for the lie that you will look desperate if you dedicate time to pray for your future spouse. That is not true. The devil will concoct any lie to stop you from praying for such a crucial life matter. The world will mock you for seeking out God in your love life. Do not oblige. Blessed are you who seeks out God on every matter. You are saving yourself a lot of heartache. The Lord encourages us to pray about everything and anything that makes us anxious (See Phil 4:6). Beloved, be released from the devil's snare. He seeks to take you down with reproach. He very loudly offers up unsolicited comments with the aim of backing you into a small corner of shame. You know his suggestions:

- Your friends are getting married, what is wrong with you? Maybe you are cursed?
- Look at her, that is her third boyfriend and you haven't received any male attention in a while

- You may be wife material but there are no men who want to court you
- You lack opportunity
- Getting hitched has never been this difficult
- What do you know about men? Can you even keep a man?

You may be thinking, "Well, I've heard that from my relatives and not the devil" Well, sometimes people are insensitive. The bottom line is, if it is not emanating from the Father's heart, don't let it settle in your heart. God will not torture you with doubt, comparison or self-hatred. God does not find it silly that you are praying for a spouse now more than ever because you want to get married.

In addition, it is also vital that you pray similarly for a spouse as you would for any other burning request. If you climb the mountain, fast or hold special prayers when something is immensely bothering you, do the same as you pray for your future husband. You can plan to dedicate a couple of days to pray for your future spouse. Don't let shame stop you. Pray until you are satisfied and the matter is settled in your heart. If you seek divine intervention on other matters why not this? Prayer is powerful— at the feet of Jesus you can lay it all down. The One who is able. You can take everything off your chest and cast it all on Jesus.

At the end of the day, you know the quality of marriage you seek. You know any man is not the right one. You know the cost of choosing the right partner. It is a major decision that will affect the rest of your life. It will have an impact on your future, your career, your children and everything concerning you. Marriage is *that* serious and it requires from you, an investment in prayer.

IT'S ANXIETY TALKING

What is anxiety saying about your current situation and future relationship?

- If I embrace being single I will enjoy it too much and it will keep me from putting myself out there
- No ideal man will notice me in these type of clothes

- I will probably end up with someone I don't like
- I should accommodate any guy just in case he is the one
- What if I am not good enough for him?
- What if we end up getting a divorce in the future?
- If I don't put myself out there I won't get noticed
- I should have an exact description of the guy I want otherwise God won't give me anyone I like
- Did I hear God right?
- I shouldn't plan for my future too much just in case my future spouse has different life plans
- What if our values, goals, dreams, and beliefs don't align?
- My attitude stinks, how can anyone put up with me?
- I need to fix myself for someone to love me

Do such perplexing thoughts ever make you feel like screaming out, "shut up!?" It can be really frustrating. What are some of your anxieties? I may not have included them in the list above but you know everything that bothers you. I would encourage you to list them down. Honestly list them down, there are certain things that we push to the back of our minds because we feel ashamed to admit even to ourselves that they make us uncomfortable. List them down anyway; no-one has to see them, you can keep it between you and God. I'll show you in the next section what you should do once you've listed them down.

TAKE THEM DOWN ONE BY ONE

There is nothing that the Bible does not have a solution for. This is what Paul told Timothy about the Scriptures, *"All Scripture is God-breathed and is useful for teaching, rebuking, correcting, and training in righteousness so that the man of God may be thoroughly equipped for every good work"* (Timothy 3:16). For whatever you need, the Word of God will prove useful to you. I believe that marriage is a ministry and it has to produce good works. For you to be thoroughly equipped for this good work you need to know the Scriptures.

Like me, you probably don't know **all** the Scriptures but you for sure know some. Use the ones that you know and be intentional in learning more (you could also make use of Google). For every anxiety that you've listed down find Scripture that addresses that specific problem. You could pick one or more Scriptures for each one of the anxieties you've listed down.

Here is an example of how you could do it:

Anxiety: I don't know if I will ever get married; it is taking too long

Counter-attack: I know God will bring my life partner at the right time (Isaiah 60: 22). God knows exactly what I desire; he cares about what I desire (Psalm 37:4) and he takes pleasure in my success (Psalm 35:27). My desires will come to pass; I choose to take pleasure in God (Psalm 37:4) for he is good (Psalm 136:1). I choose to be hopeful because I believe in his love for me (1 John 4: 16).

Verses:

- "And so we know and rely on the love God has for us."(1 John 4:16)

- "Take delight in the LORD, and he will give you the desires of your heart."(Psalm 37:4)

The two verses above serve as an example to show you how you can derive certain truths from the Scriptures. It doesn't have to be so many Scriptures even one is fine as long as it deals with the specific anxiety you are struggling with.

IDENTIFYING THE VOICE OF GOD

It can be very difficult to isolate the voice of God within a whirlwind of anxious and conflicting thoughts. I have come to learn that fellowship with God is bound by peace. He is merciful and kind. In his presence, there is the fullness of joy. Whatever is accusatory, full of condemnation and doubt, does not come from him. The Bible says that the Holy Spirit convicts us of righteousness (John 16: 8-11 NKJV). If you, feel ashamed, that you are not good enough or that you are a disappointment, it's not from God.

Learn to distinguish the voice of the liar and accuser from the voice of our heavenly Father. The only way you can do that is if you become familiar with the Father's voice. In the same way, you would identify your mother or sister's voice in a crowd, you should confidently know God's voice. Jesus said that *"Sheep know the shepherd's voice....they run away from a stranger because they don't recognize a stranger's voice"* (see John 10: 4-5). He was referring to himself as the shepherd (see John 10: 11) and believers are his sheep.

Sheep follow their shepherd, just as we like to be around the people we know love us, as a matter of fact, we cling to them. On the other hand, we evade those with bad intentions who are out to hurt us. God does not seek to harm you. He is full of mercy, grace, and love. His intentions for you are good.

Therefore, if whatever you believe is opposite to all that the Scriptures say about God then there must be an error in what you are hearing. You have a Father who loves you and if he *"...did not spare his own Son, but gave him up for us how will he not also, along with him, graciously give us all things?"* (Romans 8:32). Always remember that you are loved and this was already demonstrated many years ago on the cross (see 1 John 4: 9-10). You can reflect on the cross as many times as you need as a reference point when you want to be assured of God's love for you.

Drown the negative voices in your head by taking every thought that crosses your mind captive to the obedience of Christ. Filtering your thoughts through the understanding of the love God has for you (1 john 4:1). The ability to separate what God is saying from all the other voices in your head will help you put all your anxieties to rest.

WHY THE JITTERS?

I know we've all probably heard of wedding jitters where the bride or groom begins to have second thoughts over their decision to get married as the wedding day draws closer. The reasons for this form of anxiety could be caused by a number of factors. It could be the thought of the lifetime commitment to one person, fear of the in-laws and many other uncertainties. I know of people who have pulled out from weddings at the last minute because they developed cold feet. It kind of makes sense for a lifetime commitment right? I actually think any form of transition in life has the ability to make anyone nervous. Hence, it makes sense if you are having marriage jitters now even when you haven't met your life partner.

What makes you cringe at the thought of marriage? Including those thoughts or experiences that incite hatred within you towards marriage. Cast them all on Jesus. Bring your cares and concerns to him. I say this knowing full well that you are a single woman who strongly desires to be married one day. Being open to a marriage in the future does not spare you from feeling apprehensive about it.

There are so many things that happen around us, especially as women that have distorted our view of marriage. One story on the news would make you want to take down the vision board you created for your wedding, tear it up and throw it in the bin. Have you ever considered the things that make you tick when it comes to marriage?

There are things that you may feel the need to prevent from happening in the future marriage that you have seen affect other marriages. Some of you may have been exposed to the dysfunction in your own parent's marriage. Recognising some of the ugly details of what goes on in your parents' marriage, who have served as your initial example of marriage may make you cringe at the thought of the outcome of your own marriage.

Anyone could give so many negative reasons why you shouldn't aspire to get married and you would probably convince a jury without reasonable doubt. However, if summoned, would you make a sound case for couples whose marriages serve as exemplary?

Obviously, no couple is perfect but if you could list down at least those that you consider ideal, how many names would you have on your list? Go ahead and try it. Indeed, some of you probably wouldn't have your own parents on the list nor your close family members. I am not stating this to say there are no good marriages. Good marriages exist. I believe God's goodness supersedes all the bad in this world. I am positive there is a large remnant of good marriages in this world that God has set apart for himself. I am personally rooting for your marriage to be the many good ones that will be exemplary to the future generations!

In light of all the fears, have you ever considered why you keep aspiring for marriage? I present to you that it is God's design. The One who uniquely crafted you and placed the good desire for marriage in your heart is the reason you continue to aspire towards marriage. I believe that God's design for marriage including the path towards marriage is not complicated. God's design is simple and beautiful. Never once has God set his children up for disaster. Not once! Fear not. Keep that vision board, don't throw it away.

Be encouraged today because God cares about whatever makes you afraid. There is no condemnation. The things would definitely overwhelm your mind. The little (and big) things: issues concerning how you will raise your kids; the feelings that drive you back to the drawing board when you had made strides of faith into a hopeful future. Lay them all before the Lord. God waits for you to surrender your fears to him to help you overcome them. He has all the answers. He knows just what to do and say to calm your nerves. He will put your fears to rest with his perfect love. He is not even surprised when you possess certain fears. They can come in every size, and shape. They will not make him uncomfortable. If not to him then to whom will you take your cares?

THE CAPACITY TO LOVE

The idea of spending the rest of your life with someone for as long as you live could feel weighty. We all come from different family backgrounds and are accustomed to a particular way of life. Imagine living with someone who doesn't value birthdays as much as you do? I imagine how sometimes I can't even plan for my own birthday; how then would I plan for somebody else? The idea of constantly buying gifts for one person for the rest of your life seems like work. But that's just me. You might be a great planner and you've got gifting down. However, you might have other things that irk you at the thought of consistently giving a lifetime of love to one individual. Even the thought of adjusting your schedule to include another person is cringe-worthy.

It might be your personality. Maybe you are irritable towards certain things and considering your temperament when provoked, you are appalled at the thought of reacting the same way to your future spouse.

I believe there is an underlying fear of all these thoughts you have when you imagine your capacity to love. It is simple. You fear that you don't qualify as someone who is worthy of undying devotion. You will view your significant other in the same way, as a person not deserving of unconditional love.

The fear of "I can't". "Lord, I can't love him". "Lord, he won't love me". The thought that one day your love for your spouse will run out and that he will also stop loving you. *Disposable. Not Irreplaceable.*

"We love because he first loved us"[1]— on your own you don't have the capacity to love. Love is not something that is derived from within us. As believers, we are blessed to be covered by the love of God that infiltrates human relationships. *Flawed. Inexperienced.* Human relationships. The love of God is the glue that joins together two flawed human beings and presents them as holy and blameless.

Practice won't keep your man. Years of experience might just fail you. Your "bomb" personality just won't cut it. It does not work that way. Unless God is in it. Only, with the help of the Holy Spirit and by his step by step leading then can you love right. I am sure life will be easier for you by his leading.

You, girl, will have this marriage thing down! You've got this! God's yoke is easy and his burden is light. Be assured that the godly relationship you are awaiting will be God's version of easy. There are relationships that are difficult and complicated, to be honest, I can't keep up with them. There are ladies who are analysing activities and words said by their love interest just to figure out if they are an official couple. That must surely be stressful. I know with God-initiated relationships, you won't be left guessing. Everything will be intentional. There will be no need for you to be weighed down by analysis, dissections or calculations. It will be unforced and *easy*—love shouldn't be a struggle.

THINK GOOD THOUGHTS

The Biblical perspective of our thought life is very challenging. After reading some verses on thoughts I realised it was much more serious than I thought. Here, let's look at some of my favourites:

- A good man brings good things out of the good stored up in his heart, and an evil man brings evil things out of the evil stored up in his heart. For the mouth speaks what the heart is full of. (Luke 6:45)
- As a man thinks so he is (Proverbs 23:7)
- May the words of my mouth and the meditation of my heart be pleasing in your sight (Psalm 19:14)
- We take captive every thought to make it the obedient to Christ (2 Corinthians 10:5)

This particular verse stands out from my personal favourites. Philippians 4:8: *"Finally brothers and sisters, whatever is true, whatever is noble, whatever is right, whatever is pure, whatever is lovely, whatever is admirable— if anything is excellent or praiseworthy— think about such things."*

The NKJV translation of the same verse replaces the word think with meditate. To meditate is defined as: to think deeply, study or turn something over and over in your head. Whenever I encounter the word, meditate, I'm immediately reminded of Joshua 1: 8 which says, *"Keep this Book of the Law on your lips; make sure you meditate on it day and night, so that you are careful to do everything that is written in it."* There is a direct link between meditating and doing. Whatever you allow to enter and occupy your mind will reflect in your life. The things you do are a result of how you think even on the days you claim that you did something "without thinking."

Craig Groeschel shared that "your life moves in the direction of your strongest thoughts."[2] This statement should make you *think* and consider some of your strongest thoughts. Are the majority of your thoughts leaning towards the negative or positive side? You have to monitor your thoughts and become intentional about having a good thought life.

For someone who has struggled with anxiety, I know the damage anxious thoughts will have on the perspective you have of yourself and others. I remember walking into rooms and I would judge what people thought of me by their looks. I would freak out thinking, "oh they probably think what I am wearing is ugly" and sometimes I would wonder if they thought I was cool enough or pretty enough to sit with them. My mind was constantly crowded with hypotheticals of what other people thought about me.

Eventually, I realised that no one has the superpowers that allow them to read other people's minds and deduce what they are thinking at any given time. However, each individual can choose which thoughts they entertain and allow to occupy their mind.

Thinking good thoughts is medicine for the anxious heart. Have you ever found yourself overthinking a statement said to you by someone else? Picture this: A certain guy shows an interest in you. You tell your friend and she says to you, "That guy flirts with everyone" how do you react to that? Do you start questioning your worth? As in does that mean I'm not cute after all? Did he mean what he said or was he just saying that to flatter me? And there begins an endless spiral of suppositions.

I want you to consider how you could incorporate Phil 4:8 into your thought life. Use it as a filter perhaps for all your unwanted thoughts. The truths in this verse will usher you into having peace of mind. Transfer this way of thinking to how you view dating and marriage. That way, you are conditioning yourself to have a positive perspective regarding marriage— eliminating all forms of negativity and as a result, you will also have peace in that area. The peace that surpasses all understanding. People will wonder why you don't yield to the increasing pressure you are receiving from the world. You would have trained yourself to see the world with a godly perspective from the riches of Philippians 4:8 which will leave you calm and unshakeable. With your mind made up, it will be difficult to offend you.

Another point I want to make is that, think good thoughts about your future. When your mind is creating, lean towards making good memories. What are some of your strongest thoughts towards marriage?

Do you find it easier to embrace negative thoughts? Do you know that it is okay, to think good thoughts? It is not being too overly ambitious or wishful thinking. Your thoughts matter. You will have to be intentional about having a good thought life. Consider everything that crosses your mind to be a suggestion and before any suggestion lands to occupy space in your brain examine it against what is dictated in God's Word.

CHAPTER FIVE

GROW IN FAITH

"Continue to live your lives in him, rooted and built up in him..."
Colossians 2: 6-7

At the core of our faith is believing in Christ Jesus (See Rom 10: 8-10). A new life began the moment you made Jesus Christ your Lord and Saviour. For that reason, your growth as a believer is of great importance just as a baby's development. The same way you would find it unusual and upsetting to witness a baby's growth becoming stagnant, it is absolutely unusual for you as a believer to stop growing. You should never become complacent with the existing knowledge you have of the Word of God. You can never know enough for eternity, you have to keep growing.

The following Bible verse is one of the most quoted verses with regards to women: *"Charm is deceptive, and beauty is fleeting but a woman who fears the LORD is to be praised"* (Proverbs 31: 30). Only a woman who fears the Lord must have made him master over her affairs. If you are that kind of woman, you are worthy of praise. What kind of woman are you becoming? What sort of wife do you want to be? Think of it this way: a wife that fears the Lord brings praise to her husband. I don't know about you but one day I want to represent my family well, wherever I go. Your faith in this season will play a vital role in refining your desired goals as a married woman. Your faith will contribute to what you believe about yourself. Faith gives you the confidence that is necessary for empowering you to be the best version of yourself. Your faith will also determine the quality of your transition into marriage. By faith, you can be sober-minded and make good decisions concerning your future. Ultimately, faith will change you into the ideal person you want to be. Your faith in Jesus has the transformative power to help you drop harmful attitudes and practices which could destroy your relationships.

FEED TO GROW

God is the only one responsible for the spiritual growth that we experience in our lives (1 Corinthians 3: 6). One of the ways that God helps us grow is through his Word. As we hear the Word of God your faith increases (Rom 10:17). Having said that, what do you spend a lot of time listening to? Is it your favourite love song? Views from a talk show? Or a certain channel on YouTube? If hearing the Word of God can contribute to your faith then without a shadow of doubt whatever else you spend time listening to will also have an influence on you.

Growing up, I enjoyed listening to break-up songs, especially those sung by female artists. I used to sing them with such heartfelt passion as if I was going through an actual break-up. I generally just had a liking for these songs. But later on, I realised that it was more than casual listening that was taking place. I was really taking the lyrics of every song to heart and it influenced my perspective of men so much so that if I had a boyfriend at that time, I don't think our relationship would have survived. I had subconsciously accepted that men would inevitably disappoint and hurt their partners and they were not to be trusted.

You need to heed this: behind every voice, there is a person who holds their own opinions, values, and personal beliefs. And with their words, people often communicate these opinions, values, and beliefs. Therefore, you need to be aware of what is being communicated, for communication has the power to appeal to your emotions, influence your judgment and if it is negative, can defer your hope. What beliefs are held by the person you are listening to? Do their beliefs align with the

Word of God? Are they Spirit-led? What fruit are their words producing in your life?

When you feed on God's Word, you can be guaranteed that you will grow in your faith. There is a ripple effect that happens as you spend more time in God's Word—you draw closer to God and as you draw closer to God, you begin to adopt his values and live by his principles which will inevitably make you a better person. When you are familiar with God's ways, the worldly conduct will be strange to you, and you will be able to distinguish what is and what is not of God.

DON'T STOP GROWING

In your pursuit of education, you start learning from pre-school, then move on to primary school, secondary school and finally you pursue tertiary education. Learning becomes more advanced as you move from one level of attainment to another. In the same way, you need to advance in the learning of the Word of God. This is what Paul had to say in Hebrews 5:12, *"... though by this time you ought to be teachers you need someone to teach you the elementary truths of God all over again."* This clearly shows that at some point the Hebrews stopped growing. Imagine having obtained a university degree but with the knowledge of a pre-schooler? Clearly, something must have gone wrong and everyone around you will begin to notice especially your prospective employers.

What I am trying to get at is this; you need to see the value of every opportunity you get to learn the Word of God. You don't want to be left behind without having acquired the necessary knowledge for the seasons ahead. It is imperative that you find out whatever is distracting you from growing and resolve it to avoid any undesirable outcomes.

I've witnessed women who are believers, but because they stopped growing made drastic mistakes. For instance, if you are grown you would know that marrying a guy just because you met him at a church does not make him husband material! You intentions are to grow old with this man, you can't afford to make such silly mistakes. A grown woman would know that a man won't change his despicable behaviour on account that you've tied the knot. You are only setting yourself up for heartache. What you encounter during courtship will be what you encounter in marriage. If he was flirtatious with other women before you were married he will continue to be flirtatious into your marriage. If he did not respect you while you were dating what makes you think that's going to change in marriage?

It's the deliberate and frequent use of the Word of God that will cause you to grow in your faith. The Bible says, *"Do not let this book of the law depart from your mouth, meditate on it day and night so that you may be careful to do everything written it"* (Joshua 1:8). What the Book of the Law was to Joshua is what the Bible is to us. You have to treasure the words inscribed in the Bible to ensure that you are equipped with relevant knowledge for every season.

AS YOU GROW

1) YOUR MIND IS RENEWED

"Be transformed by the renewing of your mind" (Romans 12:2). Before we were saved our minds were carnal. There are lies that you may have grown up believing, you might have been so convinced of these lies which eventually, settled in your heart and became a part of you. Now that you know the Truth, you need a complete overhaul of the beliefs you previously held in exchange for godly ones. However, it's not a task that could be done within a day and it requires commitment. When you are convinced of a lie the truth appears false. For that reason, you need to spend more time in the Word of God to propel that change in your life.

One of the lies I believed was that there was no relationship free of drama. If you have watched some Malawian drama series, Tyler Perry movies, or Love and Hip Hop, you would understand. So, I used to prepare myself for the drama that would inevitably ensue in my future relationship. As I began to regularly read the Word of God the lies attached to this erroneous belief were exposed. It was one particular verse that was an eye-opener for me, it said, *"Aim to be at peace with* ***everyone*** *(see Romans 12:18)."* "Everyone" includes my future spouse right? I like to think so, and that's why I believe in a drama-free relationship. No relationship consisting of two imperfect people is spared from disagreements but that does not mean they cannot be amicably resolved. I pray you begin to let go of the "soap-opera" type of love and embrace the Christ-like love.

2) YOU BECOME WISE

Paul continued to tell the Hebrews that, *"Solid food is for the mature who by constant use have trained themselves to distinguish good from evil"* (Hebrews 5: 14). Wisdom is the act of distinguishing good from evil. As you study and learn from the Word of God, you become more acquainted with what is good. The Lord's ways become incorporated into your lifestyle. You begin to adopt the Lord's nature. So if you were an angry person, you learn how to become one who is slow to anger (James 1:19); you develop a quiet and gentle spirit (1 Peter 3:4) replacing your restless heart. I truly believe, wisdom guides you into better decision making, especially concerning what to value and what to discard.

Furthermore, it also teaches you to apply knowledge accordingly. One of the things I've learnt and has proven to be vital from my fellowship with the Holy Spirit is to have a sound mind. Sometimes, we mindlessly pursue relationship matters and end up forfeiting crucial knowledge. Even you can be unwise in your choice of information by deeming crucial information as useless when it would have very well guided you. For instance, I remember the many times I would zone out during a church service if the sermon was on marriage. In my thinking, this sermon did not apply to me so I did not see the need to listen. There are definitely certain messages that are strictly for married people but there also some lessons from sermons on marriage that every individual could learn from.

On the other extreme, you may have become interested only in the content on marriage and now that's the only message you prioritise. Again, you could also miss out on vital seasonal teachings that would enrich your life. Even more dangerously, you could end up inappropriately applying in your singleness the information strictly reserved for a married woman. For instance, I've personally witnessed women act as wives especially with their acts of service to men (not their boyfriends nor prospective husbands) because they want to be credited as dutiful and therefore eligible wives. Women like those could use the special attribute of the Holy Spirit which enables you to possess good judgement. This new way of thinking allows you to place more value on things as God requires you, in each season. It keeps you from getting ahead of yourself and it allows you to embrace every season as it comes.

INTIMACY

You are a child of God first before you are a woman, a daughter, an employer, an employee, a mother, a sister or a friend. Before you take up all these responsibilities, your first priority is to be preoccupied with the affairs of your heavenly father. You may be familiar with this verse, 1 Corinthians 7: 34, *"An unmarried woman or virgin is concerned about the Lord's affairs: her aim is to be devoted to the Lord in both body and spirit."* This privilege applies to you, up until the time you become a wife. Singleness is truly a gift because you get to know God without diverting your attention towards other tasks that you would undertake after becoming a wife. In a literal sense the "wife package" includes besides your day job, daughter in law duties, home management, and you will eventually take on the role of mummy which also extends to being a doctor who is always on call, a chauffeur, chef, and tutor. Whatever tasks you are juggling now are fewer in comparison to what you will eventually take on once "he puts a ring on it." Yes, the ring you want so badly. I promise my intention is not to scare you. I am only putting things into perspective. Life will only get busier for you. You need to appreciate the extra time you have for yourself that allows you to spend more time with God.

You would take your time if you knew the value of cultivating a deep relationship with the Lord. There were two sisters, Mary, and Martha who hosted Jesus and his disciples at their home when they came to their village. A fascinating incident happened: Martha was so busy working and preparing food for the guests, all the while, Mary was with Jesus listening to what he was saying. Martha was greatly bothered by this and she proceeded to call out Jesus for permitting Mary not to help her with the work. Jesus's response to Martha was rather fascinating and

I will particularly focus on the last part of what he said to her. He said, *"Only one thing is needed and Mary has chosen what is better and it will not be taken from her."*[1]

Consider Mary at the feet of Jesus, the desire to be in his presence and to hear his Word. Her hunger to know him. Jesus is all that mattered. It's that closeness that grew her love and trust in Jesus. In Psalm 27:4, *"David said, one thing I ask from the Lord, this only do I seek: that I may dwell in the house of the Lord all the days of my life, to gaze upon the beauty of the Lord and to seek him in his temple."* David's words resonate with what Jesus said to Martha. There's only **one thing** that matters for you too, darling. And it's to know Jesus and to spend more time in his presence. It's so important that you know God for yourself. In the same way, you become so closely in sync with your friends; you ought to develop that same intimacy with God. There is a confidence that comes by knowing God that will get you through anything. As you get to know God more and more, a stronger bond is created.

You were created for a relationship. At the core of who you are is what you believe about God and what you believe about yourself. There is absolutely no substitute for knowing God, especially now while you are still single. Well-formed identity can only come out of believing that you are his beloved. Knowing and embracing this will affect your entire outlook on life.

Darling, your heavenly Father is interested in your life. He wants you to spend quality time with him and share with him everything about your life. He also wants you to keep an ear out for his voice. As much as you may desperately want to leave this unmarried life, you will never get this time back. You have to invest in finding out who you are in Christ as an individual and understanding how this relationship shapes your life. Now is the appropriate time for you to squeeze out all these single lady privileges.

It's so vital that your devotion to the Lord remains your priority for as long as you are single. The transformation you will witness as you spend more time with the Lord will affect every area of your life. I believe it will be easier to maintain your devotion to the Lord in your capacity as a wife because you would have already made God integral in your own life. What you learn while you are still single creates a foundation that you can build upon while you are in courtship and eventually in marriage. Your relationships, your work ethics, your parenting, and all the affairs of your life will hinge on your faith. Don't wait until you are married to become devoted to God. It starts now. Go ahead and maximise on your single years.

CHAPTER SIX

TAKE GOD AT HIS WORD

Let us hold unswervingly to the hope we profess for he who promised is faithful

Hebrews 10:23

The Scripture in Psalms18: 30 says, *"As for God, his way is perfect; the word of the LORD is flawless..."* This verse has helped me in shifting the way I think about God's promises to his children. I've embraced the truth that God won't lead us to an undesirable ending. I'll also be the first one to let you know that it doesn't always feel that way when you can't see results, you don't feel God near and your prayers seem to go unheard. You will find yourself in a conundrum when you believe God has promised you one thing and yet experience a situation that seems contradictory to his Word. It applies to everyone and I hope this resonates with you too.

Let's be honest, our faith in an invisible God gets tested. It would actually be easier to believe in the things that we can see and fully comprehend. Yet, that's the beauty of our faith in the Lord Jesus. The same way you believed in him by faith and made him your Lord and Saviour and witnessed a change in your life; you can likewise expect him to be present— here and now. He is always working on your behalf. He is not about to fail you or ignore your call.

LIVE BY FAITH

When you observe the hall of faith in Hebrews 11, you will discover that God's faithfulness works well together with our faith. When we are unfaithful, God still remains faithful (2 Timothy 2:13) but it is more pleasing to God when we have faith (Hebrews 11:6). If there is work that God wants you to do— the easy yoke and light burden, is, to believe (Matthew 11: 28-30). When you think about it, faith is simply taking God at his Word. Words are invisible and this becomes crucial when someone makes a promise, since all you can rely on is the person's word, without really knowing their actual intentions. They could easily change their mind or they could be lying. This could become worrisome for you if God is the promisor and you don't know the nature of God.

Hebrews 11:1, in the Message translation, says, *"The fundamental fact of existence is that this trust in God, this faith, is the firm foundation under everything that makes life worth living. It's our handle on what we can't see."* Since we've brought up this verse, you know things just got serious. And, yes, marriage is still the topic of discussion:

As a believer faith is your reason and your strength for getting up each morning. You gain confidence through your faith in Jesus. Faith is bold and exists as your weapon against fear. Within oneself, you might feel both fear and faith simultaneously. If recognised and utilised, faith will crush fear.

It would be beneficial to you if you believed in God's Word more than you grumble and complain. I say this, knowing full well how much time women could spend discussing problems without offering up any solutions. *Girl chats.* You take turns in lamenting. Sometimes, you are well aware of what God has said about a matter but you choose to complain anyway. Let's say, you knew that for a season you had to remain absolutely single. However, along the way, you decided otherwise and began to pray for God to send you a spouse at that moment. What response would you expect from God? Living by faith will require you to remember and refer back to God's initial Word concerning a specific matter.

Maybe some (probably most of us) didn't get a clear word from God regarding marriage. However, constant interaction with the Word of God may have brought about a certain understanding and you have picked up on verses that directly address your concerns. For example, you may be meditating on a verse like Psalms 84:11, *"God will withhold, no good thing,"* but you feel like God is hesitant in bringing your husband. We can deduce from this verse that, if God does not withhold anything good from you then he is not hindering you from meeting your husband.

It is vital that you act out what you believe. One practical way to do that is by speaking it out. You need to speak in line with what you believe according to 2 Corinthians 4:13, *"He believed and therefore he spoke."* Although you may know in your mind and accept it in your hearts, you also need to hear yourself say it. Get it out of your heart and mind and onto your lips. You can easily reason away your beliefs in your mind but once you begin to voice out God's Word you won't have the chance to overthink matters and convince yourself otherwise.

WHAT IS THE NATURE OF GOD?

God is all-sufficient and because of his nature, he will meet you at your point of need. If you need a friend, he will not show up as a judge. At the same time, he does not change according to your mood. He remains constant. Sometimes, you may expect punishment from God but instead, he acts graciously. The Bible says of God, *"You do not treat us according to what our sins deserve"* (Psalm 103: 10). God acts completely based on his nature, not on your behaviour.

I've selected a few of his attributes that portray who God is:

- He is not like a man (Numbers 23:19)
- He does not lie (Numbers 23:19)
- He does not change his mind (1 Samuel 15:29)
- He is love (1 John 4:8)
- He loves you (John 16:27)
- He gives good gifts (Matthew 7:11)
- He does not keep any good thing from us (Psalm 84:11)
- He freely gives us all things (Romans 8:32)
- He removed our sin as far as the East is from the West (Psalm103:12)

- He is the ancient of days (Daniel 7:9)
- He is mindful of you (Psalm 8:4)
- When you ask, he hears you (1 John 5: 14-15)
- He cares for you (1 Peter 5:7)
- He perfects everything concerning you (Psalm 138:8)

Your confidence in God will come from understanding his nature. Why else would you get the confidence to ask God for anything concerning you unless you knew of his good nature? Surely, there must be a certain attribute of God which you know that gives you the audacity to trust him. When you know God's nature it is easy to believe his promises. Consider what you know about God and use it to conjure up the confidence you need to approach his throne.

ALWAYS FAITHFUL TO HIS PROMISE

The Psalmist in Psalm 27:5 said, *"I am confident of this, I will see the goodness of the Lord in the land of the living. Wait for the Lord; be strong and wait for the Lord."* When it comes to God, you can be sure he will come through for you; that's just how he works. You have to decide to trust him even when you can't see, and even when your answer is delayed. The truth is he will always keep his part of the deal, simply believe it. This will help you evade all the worrisome questions: Will it happen? Why is it not happening now? Did I do something wrong to make God retract his word? Have I missed my cue? The Scriptures in Numbers 23: 19 says, *"God is not a man, that he should lie nor a son of man, that he should change his mind. Does he speak and then not act? Does he promise and not fulfil?"*

That's God's Word for you, my friend. God's that good. He has asserted that his Word never returns to Him void, it accomplishes what it was sent to do (Isaiah 55:11). He is faithful to *his* promise. Have you ever thought of it that way? As in his promise is not based on you having to make yourself perfect before he could bless you. He is not faithful because of your actions—neither your failings nor good deeds. It hinges on his grace and mercy alone. It is about who he is. Stop trying to outdo God. If he based his faithfulness on your capabilities then you would be disqualified from plenty of good things.

What are some things you feel disqualify you:

- I have a child
- I am not pretty enough
- I can't cook
- I am not a virgin
- I am no longer young
- I am antisocial

Well, praise be to God for he is an expert at taking the least things of the world and making them. *"He takes the foolish things of the world and makes them wise to shame those in the world who consider themselves wise"* (1 Corinthians 1:27). Jesus is the kindness and love of God towards man who saved the worst people—disobedient fools stumbling in darkness. He saved us according to his mercy and not by any righteous works we have done.[1] You never earned his love and mercy then—when you didn't know but needed it the most. Why would he forsake you now that you are part of his family? I'm telling you God is revered for taking a chance on indifferent people including those with a bad reputation. What is impossible with man is possible with God.

You may be thinking, "time has already gone, and I can't keep waiting on God. If I keep waiting on him, he will let me down." That's anxiety talking; anxiety tells you to trust in your own efforts to speed up the process rather than wait on God. That's a well-decorated lie from the devil. Yes, sometimes it may take longer than you anticipated but it is never to hurt or harm you. It is always for your good.

The Psalmist, in Psalm 130:6 states, *"I will wait for the Lord, more than the watchman waits for the morning, more than the watchman waits for the morning."* Has there ever been a time in your life when the morning never came? If you have ever employed a security guard at your residence you know very well that they always look forward to the dawning of a new day. As soon as dawn breaks, they pack up their things and leave. If watchmen are able to determine the dawn of a new day through their daily experience, how about you, child of God? You should be more convinced of God's faithfulness who you know makes possible the rising of the sun, each and every day.

KEEP HANGING ON TO THE WORD

Psalm 119: 109 says, *"The Word of God is a light unto my path and a lamp unto my feet."* As a believer, the Word of God should be your ultimate guide through life. You need to make a deliberate choice to uphold the Word of God in your decision making overall life's issues. You have to be a doer of the Word even if the world suggests otherwise. You are in this world but not of it. So when it comes to relationships you cannot let the media, society or your misguided friends define your stance. Faith in God should be your drive. What's going to happen if no one is talking about "practicing abstinence" or "Waiting on God for a spouse?" Or if people are talking but are speaking in contrast to your beliefs?

I have found myself in the middle of such discourse. I certainly felt as if I was exaggerating my beliefs concerning my love life because even some of my own Christian friends were not embracing their faith to the extent that I was. However, I held on to the truth that God's opinion about love and waiting on Him to direct our steps still remained the same.

I came across 1 John 1:26-27 and it stood out to me. I particularly like the Message translation of this verse: *"I've written to warn you about those who are trying to deceive you. But they're no match for what is embedded deeply within you - Christ's anointing, no less! You don't need any of their so-called teaching. Christ's anointing teaches you the truth on everything you need to know about yourself and him, uncontaminated by a single lie. Live deeply in what you were taught."*

In as much as the context of this verse was referring specifically to the presence of the antichrist, it contains profound truths that are useful to your life as unmarried women. You would agree with me that people say a lot and also omit some things about relationships but either way, they leave you confused and wondering, "What should I believe?"

Well, you have the Truth— the Word of God. You may feel alone because of the numerous opinions heralded at you which completely oppose God's Word. Think of the idea of having a child outside wedlock. The world has painted it as "traditional" to have children born within the confinements of marriage. It is considered normal these days if you never get married and still plan to have biological children. Society approves of the couple that finds themselves unexpectedly pregnant outside of marriage as long as they eventually get married. This sounds absolutely normal according to worldly standards. I have friends and family who found themselves in the situations stated above. I still celebrated with them on the birth of their child. Children are a gift from God. And I've celebrated the marriage union of a couple who already had children prior to their wedding. But that still does not make it acceptable before God. And it will never be ok. God intended for sex to be between married people. That will never change and that is the lifestyle I choose to follow.

Know this, opinions are fleeting; God's Word is constant. Some opinions are simply sugar-coated lies and they are no match against Christ's anointing. As the verse above says, "the anointing is deeply embedded in you." **Whatever** you need to know the anointing will teach you. A lot has been shared in this book about embracing God's plan for your life regarding marriage and how to handle your personal fears and desires. The anointing will teach you about that too.

"Uncontaminated by any lie"— if you were wondering which version of "truth" to believe, how about trusting the one that is pure and unaltered? There are no half-truths here. Rest assured you will be exposed to the truth that sets people free. Let me warn you that this goes against the mantra that you've known and probably cited all your life that "the truth hurts." You may have known truth as abstract, but darling, Truth has always been a person and his name is Jesus. In the presence of Jesus, there is the fullness of joy!

The verse ends with an instruction, "Live deeply in what you were taught." What you learn from the Word of God about marriage, love, and purity is the most trustworthy information that exists. All you have to do now is live **deeply** in it. Don't ever let go of those teachings. Hold on to them dearly as if it were your life! Let God's Word be true and everything else a lie. Better yet, be so rooted in God's Word so that you easily rebuff the lies.

Deliberately choose to stand on the Word of God even if what you hear from other well-meaning people is different. There are people with good intentions who insist on offering their unsolicited views and advice—those relatives, the neighbour, even your church friends. In addition to that, philosophies valued by the world may distract you from the principles presented in God's Word. However, don't let the world's perspective on matters distract you from God's *good and perfect* will for your life. Place the Word of God as central in your life and everything else will make sense.

YOU DON'T GO UNNOTICED

Do you know God knows exactly how you feel? So when you think, he is not responding or he is deliberately ignoring you; he is actually focused on you and has not lifted his eyes off you the whole time. Martha once asked Jesus if he cared because she felt her good works were being overlooked (See Luke 10: 38-42). Have you ever felt that way? You may say, "Lord, I've been praying, I've been faithfully serving you. Can't you just give me the one thing that I want, I am not asking too much of you, I just want a husband."

The Scriptures say, *"God honours those who honour him before men"* (1 Samuel 2:30). You are probably among the seemingly few women who aim at pleasing God in every area of their lives including their love life. You have placed the matter of marriage into God's hands and are grounded in the fact that you will be ready for marriage when God declares your readiness.

Although, this is the case for you, you may feel discouraged and view it as pointless when other people do not value relationships God's way. However, the Lord notices as you believe and live out the Word while other people have shunned it. The Bible says, *"The Lord's eyes are on his children, watching over them day and night"* (Psalm 34:15). The Lord is not only concerned about providing you with protection but as he looks over you, he is also taking note of your faith.

Faith gets God's attention. You may be familiar with the story that Matthew narrates about the woman who suffered from an issue of blood for twelve years and believed that if she touched the hem of Jesus's cloak, she would be healed (Mathew 9:21). Her story is one of the many in the Gospels that tell of great faith. All throughout the Gospels, Jesus noticed and commended those that had faith.

Today, you are that person who possesses such extraordinary faith and God takes notice of you. You stand out from the crowd. In fact, God takes delight in your faith, look at Job's story. Like a proud father, God in the book of Job 2:3, unashamedly boasted about Job's faith. I don't even think Job would have imagined that his way of life could be the topic of discussion in heaven. Yet God was paying close attention to his faith. God finds faith very pleasing and it's something you should also be proud of.

On the other hand, people are observing you too, child of God. *"Creation awaits for the sons of men"* (Romans 8:19). The world is watching and waiting for you. People are excepting you to set a trend wherever you go. Whoever you are surrounded by; your family members, your friends, colleagues and fellow co-workers are all closely observing you and Christ, whom you represent. They may not say it out loud but they take notice. You are not of this world, you are a piece of a different puzzle. Therefore, you have to stick to what you believe. Don't sway from your principles about sexuality, love, marriage, and faith to accommodate contrary opinions.

AWAITING WITH EXPECTATION

There is a difference between deciding to wait on God because you are tired, frustrated and have basically given up, in comparison to waiting on God because you wholeheartedly trust him, and are not hoarding any resentment or unbelief. It is no question that our plans become frustrated but you've got to keep the faith and don't lose hope.

You should be hopeful as you wait. Hope is waiting with a sure expectation. You can declare boldly, "At the right time, God will bringing someone my way." You no longer cower in a corner when people ask you about your relationship status. When you come to a point where you can freely and unashamedly talk about your singleness and the hopes and dreams you have for your future marriage, it shows that God is perfecting a good work in you. Even when you are alone and a conflicting thoughts arises in your mind, you can still proclaim, "I'm good".

As you begin to exercise hope, you will also begin to look forward to marriage. Having laid down all your cares to God. As days go by, you are not waiting in vain. You are waiting with assured hope. Declaring, as often as possible the promises of God from his Word. Instead of being weary, you trade in the miserable "I can't wait" mantra for a hopeful new tune called, "I am looking forward to." "I am looking forward to being married." "I am looking forward to having kids," and so on and so forth. Embracing the idea that at the right time, it will happen.

CHAPTER SEVEN

WELL-SEASONED

And he shall be like a tree planted by the rivers of water that bringeth forth his fruit in season...

Psalm 1:3 KJV

Every season comes with blessings. You can cosy up to a fire in winter and on the other hand, swimming is best enjoyed in summer. Everyone lives aware of the different times of the year. We have memorised the weather conditions of each season and we make sure we have the appropriate gear to withstand every season. There are definitely times when we experience irregular seasons in the year and some may be difficult to weather, but we quickly learn to adapt to them.

This also applies to your life and spiritual journey. You need to embrace every season of life. God deliberately places you within certain environments for your own good. A place where the inherent conditions are impeccable; the perfect exertion of pressure, and a suitable temperature to help you grow. As you grow, it is inevitable that you will experience your own version of growing pains.

One of the definitions of the word *seasoned* by Chambers Dictionary is, to be rendered competent through trial and experience. There couldn't be a more precise meaning. This accurately describes what we go through as Christians. To be rendered competent is a sign of growth. Most assuredly, growth comes through passing tests, gaining experience and overcoming challenges.

THE MAN JOSEPH

There is a story about a young man named Joseph that is found in the Bible. Joseph's experience is humbling and I believe his story is a great illustration of how to live fully present in the period between a God-given dream and its realisation. It's a story of perseverance, character transformation, overcoming pain and God's faithfulness.

Joseph was a boy when he was given a dream. Just like any frivolous boy given a God-sized dream would, Joseph boasted about his dreams to his father and brothers. His brothers already hated Joseph for being their dad's favourite son and they hated him, even more, when he told them about his dreams. One day Joseph's father, Jacob sent Joseph to check on his brothers at the field where they had gone to feed their father's flock. When Joseph's brothers saw him coming from a distance and as he approached, they plotted to kill him. Led by these murderous inclinations, the brothers seized Joseph. But one of Joseph's brothers, Reuben had a change of heart and convinced the rest not to kill Joseph but to instead throw him into an empty cistern. The plans changed again and Joseph's brothers fished him out of the pit and instead sold him to the Ishmaelites who took him to Egypt where he was sold as a slave to one of pharaoh's officials, Potiphar.

One thing that stood out in the Biblical account of Joseph's story is, the Lord was with him and whatever he touched prospered[1]. His Egyptian master, Potiphar, recognized the favour on Joseph and therefore gave Joseph charge over his entire household. Yet, there was another who had her eyes on Joseph; she was Potiphar's wife. She wanted to sleep with Joseph. Joseph, being a man of God, vehemently refused day after day. One day Joseph refused her persistent advances to the point that he fled the scene leaving his cloak. She took advantage of the incident and lied that Joseph had tried to rape her. On account of this, Joseph was then thrown into prison. But even in prison Joseph still thrived with favour and he was made head over all the other prisoners.

Whilst in prison, an opportunity arose for Joseph when he correctly interpreted dreams of two men— these two prisoners were in some way closely connected to the pharaoh. A time came when the pharaoh needed his dreams interpreted and one of the two prisoners who had been released remembered Joseph. As the story goes, Joseph swapped out his prisoner clothes and put on appropriate attire worthy of a prime minister. Joseph wasn't a boy anymore, he was a man when his dreams came true. (See Genesis 37; 39; 40 and 41)

LESSONS FROM JOSEPH

A lot of women feel incomplete and think they fall short in their capacity as a woman because they don't have a man. They truly feel miserable and find themselves in a vulnerable emotional state. I am sure most women would prefer to feel secure and unbothered at all times but sometimes they are overwhelmed by discouragement and they crumble inside. This feeling resonated with me and I wondered if there was a better way. Could single women live without being inclined towards self-pity? Was it possible to be genuinely happy and enjoy every moment of singleness? Was it possible to escape loneliness and be freed from the constant feeling of not being enough? But most importantly, could unmarried women live righteously while still believing even through the painful days? You may be asking these same questions. And I present to you someone who held fast to his faith and integrity through an unfathomable series of painful life events. Here are some of the things you can learn from Joseph:

i. YOU ARE NOT ALONE

"The Lord was with Joseph". It is crucial to take into consideration this repetition that is made throughout the story of Joseph. In the pit when his own blood relatives had gotten rid of him, he was not alone. When Potiphar's wife made advances on him, he was not alone; as he worked, he was not alone. In prison, the Lord was with Joseph. You can quickly read through the story of Joseph depicted in the few chapters of the book of Genesis and immediately get the message of victory from suffering without grasping the magnitude of the events that took place over the thirteen years he was a slave. Joseph actually lived through the reality of slavery. It was real-life experience day in day out for thirteen years. This verse in Psalms gives a better picture of his situation. Psalms 105: 16-19: *"He called down famine on the land and destroyed all their supplies of food; and he sent a man before them—Joseph, sold as a slave. They bruised his feet with shackles, His neck was put in irons, till what he foretold came to pass, till the Word of God proved him true."*

The vivid account in the above verse depicts that it was not a pleasant situation for Joseph. He experienced the gruesome conditions that every slave at that time had to undergo. In the same way that God was with Joseph, he is with you child of God. He has gone before you. I understand the painful and tough situations that exist because you are single. It's real life. Struggles experienced because of singleness are more common than most women would like to admit. The constant questions and hurtful assumptions of "why you are still single at your age" can have an emotional impact on any woman. These are the same questions that leave you wondering, "Is there something wrong with me?"... "Am I cursed?" (See Chapter 4). Some seasons in life are prolonged and do not go according to plan. God understands the gravity and extremity of the conditions that you go through a single woman and he has not forsaken you.

In Psalms 23 the analogy of a shepherd and his sheep are used throughout the chapter. While I was studying the chapter, the fourth verse stood out to me, because it was different from the first three verses. The first three verses focus on the shepherd and how he leads his sheep, the fourth verse shifts the focus from the shepherd to the sheep:

"Even though I walk through the valley of the shadow of death I will fear no evil, for you are with me; your rod and staff comfort me." I am familiar with the rearing of farm animals and I know that you take the animals from the barn to a field for grazing. While at the fields the sheep are at risk of encountering predators and these beasts purposefully surround the area where sheep feed, so in some sense danger is inevitable. We too find ourselves in unpleasant situations that cannot be avoided. There is no denying that the period of waiting can be unpleasant but it also can't be avoided. Just as sheep with Jesus as your

shepherd; it is imperative that you always remember that God is with you and you can rest assured that he will see you through the difficult patches of life until you overcome and make it to the other side.

ii. ALL THINGS WILL WORKOUT FOR YOUR GOOD

When I consider how things ended for Joseph, I am truly amazed at God's ability to turn beauty from ashes. I am sure it was unheard of at that time as it would be today for a prisoner to be promoted to the prime minister. The horrible things Joseph went through for thirteen years fade in comparison to the glory that he experienced once he became prime minister. It only took one day for things to change. I was reflecting on a friend's marriage. She was the right age for marriage by the time I got to know her, but she was single and she remained that way for a while. Eventually, she got a boyfriend and later on, they got married. An exchange of vows that took place within several minutes officially transitioned her from a single lady into a married woman. The doubts that she had of ever meeting her life partner and get married were all erased in minutes. God did it.

Child of God, you are not waiting in vain. Not with our God. All things will work out for your good. Whatever shame, pain or ridicule you've experienced, should not deter you from delighting in the Lord. God is faithful. It will all work out for your good. You are on the winning team no matter how many times you fall. Are guys disappointing you over and over? Do you have a crush just to have the Holy Spirit tell you you've assigned your feelings to the wrong person? It is well. Like in the Psalm above (verses 16-17), God shut down all the food supplies of the world deliberately to create employment for this one man. He surely has already seen your way out, and it will end well for you. God is working behind the scenes in your life for your good. You will surely testify!

iii. REALISE IT'S ONLY A SEASON

Seasons were not meant to last forever. There are better things that are coming ahead (1 Corinthians 2:9). Know that even this current season you are in will end and you will come out of it victorious. I believe that Joseph knew that his life wouldn't end in prison and so this gave him the confidence to ask the cupbearer to remember him when he returned to the king's service (Genesis 40:14). Joseph still remembered the dreams God gave him as a boy; he knew the prison was only a temporary stage on his way to something bigger. Child of God, if you believe there is a possibility for marriage in the future then trust that it will happen. God is faithful. He is still fulfilling dreams and proving His Word as true.

I know some of you have spent a number of years waiting on God to bring you a spouse. You've watched your age mates get married and now you are probably witnessing those younger than you get married. God has not forgotten about you and neither have you missed your cue for marriage. It's is not easy to go through what you are going through, but I can promise you that this too shall pass. You will come out full of faith and better on the other side.

iv. FULLY EQUIPPED FOR PURPOSE

If this were a job application, this would be included in the experience section: Joseph was given leadership roles from the time he was a slave and while he was incarcerated. God knew those leadership skills would come in handy and they did. When you continue to read the story of Joseph you will discover that he was put in control over everything in pharaoh's kingdom. As a matter of fact, he was given control over the food supply of the whole world. God taught him on a small scale: taking care of household matters and taking care of his fellow prisoners. He ended up doing an exceptional job at both positions and God gave him a bigger responsibility placing him in charge of the food supply for the whole world!

What has God given you charge over, my friend? Do not despise your season, he is preparing you for something bigger. That family you have, those annoying relatives, love them because strangers will soon become your new and permanent family. I hope you believe this for God has deliberately allowed for you to be single thus far. That is why it's important to embrace the season of singleness you are currently in because whatever he equips you with now, be it skill, character or knowledge that is what is going to get you through the season of marriage. If I were you right now, I would become intentionally alert and conscious, paying attention close to the activities occurring in my life. No stage in life is meaningless, every season is purposefully designed to achieve a specific goal.

A WAY OUT

Have you ever prayed to God with a sense of urgency? This includes making prayers to God, which are expressed in the form of chants for God to change your situation at that very moment. These are the times when you are ready for heaven to literally open and drop your blessing. If one prayer doesn't work, a resolution is made to enact other prayers until all the prayers you know are fully exhausted.

I hate to admit this but I've thrown around a couple of those prayers. My prayers never ended without me demanding that it happen, now! As you may have deduced, God did not answer that prayer at that very moment. However, this is how I found peace in my situation: I surrendered to God's love, my prayer was short and sweet. I said to the Lord, *"I know you would never bring harm to me, I know you love me and I know you see me and know how I feel, you didn't buy my freedom only for me to worry, so help me persevere."*

After that prayer, I didn't want to admit this to myself but my attitude changed. My situation remained the same but I was not miserable anymore. I had the joy of the Lord, the strength of God has been present with me ever since, and I am not overcome by anxiety as before.

Sister, God knows where you are at. You might think to yourself, "God has forgotten about me, I need to remind him." "If that girl is getting married, surely something must have gone terribly wrong." No, he has not forgotten about you. Isn't the Lord the one who directs your paths? What you need to do is to ask the Lord to help you by his grace to make the best out of the season until you see God's way out. Until you see the way out, God will give you grace for each day to see the good in your singleness so that you don't come out of it miserable and bitter.

You can never be tempted beyond what you can handle; the Bible also promises that, God always creates a way out for you[2]. You have to see this as another opportunity for you to win. You should be excited. The Lord assures us that, those who put their trust in him will never be put to shame[3]. He has your best interests at heart. The Bible also says, *"Not once have I seen the righteous forsaken"* (Psalm 37:25).

"If life gives you lemons make lemonade." I am sure you are familiar with this proverb by now thanks to Beyoncé. It's a beautiful principle. It proposes that you should be optimistic although faced with an unpleasant situation. I would urge you, to ask yourself how you can contribute to God's kingdom while you are single. For example, if you are working you can use the extra money you make now (since it's not directed to other things) to bless others. Decide that you will not come out of this season empty. You don't have to wait for marriage to be happy, child of God. You can be happy now.

CHOOSE TO BE HAPPY NOW

You can cultivate joy in the wait. Paul wrote to the Philippians charging them to Rejoice in the Lord always.[4]It is easier to rejoice once you overcome a trying period, yet the Word of God still encourages you to find joy in the middle of your trials.

If you've gone hiking before you know that the climb is fun, you get to see the sunrise (depending on how early you go), you get to see the aerial view of the area where you are hiking, and the beautiful wildflowers growing along the paths. The conversation as you climb up is very enjoyable and so, of course, is taking selfies. There are also tough times— the climb can be painful, tiresome and steep. However, imagine not enjoying the climb. Imagine resorting to celebrate only when you reach the top. That would be absolutely no fun.

There will always be mountains that you have to climb in certain seasons of your life. The mountains may come as desired undertakings: the degree you need to finish, the job you need to find, the friend you need to pray for, the house you need to clean, not forgetting meeting the spouse you long for. Yet, you have the option to remain at rest while trying to accomplish any undertaking or be stressed throughout.

You will notice when hiking that it's the climb which usually has a toll on you. At the top, you can fully rest, enjoy the company of your fellow hikers, do your planned activities and eventually, you even forget about the painful part of the climb. What you need to know is that you will reach the top but you have to decide the attitude you will adopt on your way up. You could choose to be gloomy all the way or enjoy the small victories, celebrating each stride, and taking time to enjoy nature. It all depends on you: you cannot avert the process when it comes to achieving your intended goal but you can choose to be joyful during the process.

I came to a realisation in my own life that I was not enjoying the present, I always wanted to be somewhere else. I was always in a hurry. I wanted to be older, I couldn't wait to be a mum, and I couldn't wait to be a wife. Do you know what I discovered? I discovered that I could wait. I am currently waiting and in the future, I will wait when I need to. Waiting is not always fun— there are good days when you are confident to go on and days when you don't want to get out of bed. It is all part of the process, I've learnt to win on the bad days, by being optimistic and believing that everything will out work for my good.

It's not God's desire for you to worry. He says in his Word, "D*o not let your heart be troubled but trust in the Father but also trust in me*" (John 14:1). You are not justified to worry at any point in your life. There is no saying, "This is extremely bad, I could worry about this, God will understand." Nope, you can't do that. You can't choose what you can or cannot worry about.

Worry magnifies the problem beyond what it actually is. The best way to deal with a problem is not to see it using a magnifying glass but instead, with a microscopic view examine it through the lens of God's Word and see the problem the way God sees it. All the parts of the problem that make it appear so grand will shrivel right before your eyes and you will fear no more.

Instead of spending this time of singleness worrying, complaining and feeling sorry for yourself, you can spend it in a better way: enjoying the favour of God for this season; trusting the faithfulness of God and waiting with expectation. There is so much to do while waiting that you can't afford to miss out on including bettering yourself and becoming well acquainted with the Word of God.

MATURITY

Your faith will without a doubt be tested in the period of waiting. But you can find comfort in this: the experience is not in vain. The Bible says, "*Consider it much joy whenever you face trials of many kinds, because you know that the testing of your faith produces perseverance. Let perseverance finish its work so that you may be mature and complete, not lacking anything.*"[5] When you consider your period of waiting, could you say that you've grown? I observed a few things about Joseph that were different from when he was a boy. The transition was seemingly immediate. When I look at Joseph the boy and Joseph, the man, I see two different people. And the secret is hidden in his level of maturity.

1. THE DREAMER

When we are introduced to Joseph as the teenage boy, he is a brat and a show-off. He displayed proudly the dreams that God shared with him in private. He boasted of how special he was. He constantly reminded his brothers that he was not only better than them by being their father's favourite but that he would reign and rule over them, including his father and mother. Maybe Joseph did not mean to boast or show off his dreams, but because he was raised as a son set apart from among his brothers, he probably saw what he did as nothing unusual.

Once he was sold as a slave, we meet a Joseph who is more reserved. He kept to himself and only did what he was told. During his tenure at Potiphar's house, we read nothing about dreams. The next time we hear anything about dreams is when Joseph is in prison and he interprets dreams for two other prisoners. If he can interpret other people's dreams, it is apparent that Joseph also figured out the God-given dream he dreamt of as a young boy. Yet, not once did Joseph mention it to anyone at any point not even when the dream had been fulfilled.

There is a Chinese proverb that says, a seed grows with no sound. Embracing silence during trials is rather painful to our egos. Anyone would rather share their dreams or even voice out their frustrations. It's more therapeutic to tell people your desires and what you are believing for than to live in the moment. There are single women who are constantly discussing the hypotheticals of husbands, marriages, and children they don't yet have. Having such heart desires is not wrong. But sometimes it is only an escape from your present situation. We can refer back to Joseph telling his family members about his dreams and having learnt his lesson chose to keep quiet about it later on when he was a slave and as a prisoner. He faithful served in his capacity as a caretaker both when he was a slave and prisoner even though he possessed a grand God-given dream within his heart. It's so important to be level-headed by accepting where you are today as a single woman and let God bring you to the next season of life you are hoping for.

2. GET BETTER, NOT BITTER

Another thing that stands out about Joseph is that he never possessed any resentment towards anyone during his struggle or afterward. He would have easily resented God, his brothers, Potiphar, and his wife, or even the cupbearer who had forgotten him, but he didn't. Do you want to know the secret to why he didn't get bitter? Here it is: *"Do not be angry with yourselves because you sold me here, for God sent me here before you to preserve life."*[6] Perspective is everything. It's amazing that Joseph sought reconciliation with his brothers. After he had turned the events of his life over and over again in his mind, Joseph had come to the conclusion that everything happened for a *good* reason. Anyone can become susceptible to bitterness when people around them are advancing in their lives and their life feels stagnant. You see your friends getting engaged, getting married, having children and you feel resentful towards them. Yet, maturity is change from the inside out. Honestly, the most important change there is. It directly deals with your character and the way you think. The change that happens on the inside affects your external outlook on life. Come rain or sunshine you remain adamant at your core. When you stick to holding the right perspective in every situation you will be peaceful both in the middle of the season and afterward. It takes a lot of heart work on your part if you are to possess a sound mind. You need to train yourself to see the good in everything and above all to know the purpose of every season. Maturity readily recognises what God wants and quickly responds to it. Instead of looking at what would have gone wrong for you to still be single. You deliberately lift your eyes to the one who determines your seasons and ask for His will in your current situation. And when he responds you quickly attend to it.

3. GOD DEVELOPS WELL-FORMED MATURITY

God's footprints were all over Joseph's life. Joseph's fellowship with God never stopped during his struggles. And I believe it's, God's presence in his life that gave Joseph strength and hope. When we fix our eyes on God, he changes us from the inside out and brings the best out of us. He continuously works in our lives in every season and he develops in us, well-formed maturity. He fully equips you for the next season. In readiness, you go forth. The culture around you takes from you but God moulds and makes you into a better person[7]. A mature person focuses on God. You don't consistently listen out for the news or statistics of married women at your age. You would acknowledge but not obsess over the rate of divorces in your country. Maturity recognises that the season will not overwhelm you, knowing that you would not cry out, "why me?"

CHAPTER EIGHT

THE IMPORTANCE OF HAVING A VISION

Where there is no revelation people cast off restraint; but blessed is the one who heeds wisdom's instruction

Proverbs 29:18

Once in the Scriptures, the Lord encouraged the prophet Habakkuk to write down the vision (given by God) and to make it plain on tablets so that whoever read it would run with it (Habakkuk 2:1). In the same way, I believe that you should be clear about the quality of the relationship you desire. As a matter of fact, it couldn't hurt to keep a written version of your expectations; this could act as a guide as you navigate through your love life. In his book called, *Waiting and Dating*, Dr. Myles Munroe counselled against not having set principles prior to entering into a relationship. He relayed that if you entered a relationship without prior standards you would be susceptible to falling into temptation. A lot of times when you don't know what you want, you end up settling for whatever's available. Having your goals written down helps you stick to your plan especially in situations where you would find yourself compromising.

It is important to have in mind what you value in a partner with whom you would be willing to share the rest of your life and the sort of life you would build together. You have to imagine your ideal future. Think about the most valuable traits you would want your marriage to reflect. When you picture yourself married what do you see? Thinking through, writing down and voicing out what you want in a relationship is crucial. Don't be the person who accepts whatever life throws at you.

If you are afraid to imagine with the belief that you may go against God's will, don't fret. Planning for the future is not a journey anyone should undertake on their own. You will have to hear from God on the matter through his Word and prayer. As a child of God, you plan according to the revelations that God puts in your heart. As you are being led by the Spirit, he will show you the way in which you should go. Meeting your husband is part of God's plan for your life. Trust that you will be guided by his peace.

REALITY CHECK

You should at some point in your life reflect within yourself and genuinely review what you value in a relationship. As you evaluate your ideals you may discover some flaws within yourself that may trace back to certain wrong beliefs. I used to wonder if my dreams would align with the man I would marry. Somehow, I had concluded that there was no point in possessing individual ambitions with the risk that I'd eventually have to give up on my dreams to accommodate my future husband. That was a full-blown lie. It's erroneous to believe God's waiting for you to meet your life partner in order for him to start working out his purpose in your life. We've somehow equated the "commencement of life" to getting married. That is wrong because God is working within you to fulfil his will even while you are still single. There is so much you can accomplish for the kingdom of God right in the moment of your singleness. If you sincerely listed down your immediate thoughts, expectations and core values about the relationship you are believing for, what would appear on your list?
When you imagine your relationship:

- Does Christ pay an integral role in it?
- Are you happy?
- Are you settling for less than God's best?
- Are you practicing abstinence in your relationship?

- Does he believe in God?
- Are extramarital affairs in your relationship inevitable?
- Do you love him more than you love God?
- Does your relationship hinge on your performance as an individual?
- Are you free to be your authentic self?

Beginning to answer these questions puts you a step ahead in dealing with any hidden fears and misguided beliefs. As the fears and erroneous beliefs are exposed in the presence of God; God's light will begin to shine over all the dark areas. Being vulnerable even to yourself is terrifying but you have to voice out the thoughts buried deep down in your soul. It's better to release all those things that weigh you down so that God can help you process all your concerns and you can be set free.

UNCHANGEABLE PRINCIPLES FROM THE WORD OF GOD

i. TRUST GOD TO HELP YOU CHOOSE A SUITABLE COMPANION

You can trust God to help you choose your spouse. In the story of Isaac and Rebekah (Chapter 3), Eliezer prayed in his heart concerning a wife for Isaac and before he even finished praying God had already answered. God actually answered beyond Abraham's recommendations. God made sure he added to the requested package, a wife who was beautiful and a virgin. If you trust God, He will always exceed your expectations. If you trust him you can rest assured that he will give you the best.

It is such a blessing to be guided by God. We all value the advice we receive from our family and close friends : "What do you think about this guy? Do you think I should date him?" If you seek guidance from your family and close friends, you should also make an effort to hear from God, who actually knows the outcome of your impending future. Everyone needs guidance in their love life. You shouldn't leave God out of the process of figuring out the person, who you want to end up with.

ii.FLEE FROM SEXUAL IMMORALITY

You have to choose to remain pure in your relationship, mind, and body. You could be physically abstaining from sex but still have a corrupted thought life. In my experience, a common question about physical contact among adolescents is, "how far is too far?" The best answer I've heard is, "stay very far!" As a matter of fact, RUN! Don't compromise by playing on the edge. My mum always says, "it's better to be safe than sorry." I urge you to take that advice too. Practicing sexual purity requires self-control because you will be attracted to members of the opposite sex, but you have to let your inner will to please God override your feelings. You may be surrounded by people who just don't care, especially if you are in college or working. You may have friends that have "sleepovers" with their boyfriends and they make you appear overly religious when you don't allow boys over at your house or in your room at certain hours. Don't yield to the fear, stand for what you believe. You can't let your guard down, you ought to place strict measures in your life to ensure you steer clear of any sexual sin. The common Biblical advice on sexual immorality is to "Flee"[1]. You can't deliberately put yourself in compromising situations trusting that you will practice self-control if things get out of hand. Your flesh will fail you, my friend. You cannot put confidence in your flesh! It's better to avoid starting a fire than to put one out once it has been ignited.

iii.DON'T BE UNEQUALLY YOKED

"God still has sons, don't settle for a nonbeliever." This is some insight that a friend shared and it struck a chord with me. You are royalty by birth, bought with the precious blood of Jesus. You have no business mingling with those stumbling in the darkness.

Do not be fooled that there are no good Christian men. If you believe that, you will have to go outside of God's kingdom to seek a companion. God is still raising sons. There was a time when Elijah thought he was the only prophet left, but God told him, *"I have reserved seven thousand for myself who have not bowed the knee to Baal"* (See 1 Kings 19: 18, Romans 11: 3-4). It's not true that all the godly men are taken. Godly men still exist and their lives are being led by God. Refuse to water down your standards and set your eyes only on God's best. May you resolve that you will settle for nothing less than God's best.

iv.ALIGN YOUR DESIRES WITH LOVE

Marriage is a commitment to love your spouse through the good, the bad and the ugly. This goes beyond the emotional feeling of love. This love is a daily choice made in spite of your emotional state. *"Everyone will know that you are my disciples by the love you have for one another"* (John 13:35). This truth from the Scriptures extends to you and me, today. Furthermore, I truly believe that every godly marriage should exude love. As a single woman, you ought to place the commitment to love at the top of your list when considering your ideal marriage. I fear love has been put aside when envisioning marriage. Couples are placing convenience other than love at the centre of marriage—economic reasons, household care, having children and societal relevance take centre stage.

The Bible says without love we are nothing (1 Corinthians 13:2). You shouldn't be paralysed by the strong yearnings to get married that you disregard the main factor, love. Ladies, you may be well-groomed, educated, trendy, beautiful, the right age and ready to get hitched. However, if you have no intention of loving whomever you marry all that is meaningless, everything else does not qualify you for marriage. Marriage demands of us to love and receive love from another human being. You cannot overlook love as a prerequisite to govern your future marriage.

There are a lot of young couples that are getting divorced today. These are couples that are rated as cute and placed in the "#goals" category for many. In this generation where we are infatuated by "good happenings", we are not really comfortable when things don't appear picture-perfect. We believe everything should be rosy and social media worthy. The majority of the relationship goals checklists include the material things and the outward appearance of the relationship without any focus on the nitty-gritty love matters. "I want my marriage to reflect the Christ-like love" usually appears at the bottom of the checklist, if at all. His economic status, appearance, and shared fun activities are some of the qualities that take centre stage among the priorities.

My intention is not to kill your dreams of your future hubby. All those things are good and you should desire them. However, there is something much better; love. *Love never fails.* Those who love are the ones who are most qualified for marriage because through thick and thin their love will always thrive. I believe marriage is investing in a lifetime of a love-relationship. There is patience, forgiveness, sacrifice, trust, and all the attributes of 1 Corinthians 13 involved in this kind of relationship. The children and the money matters all come secondary to the commitment to love made between the husband and wife. Most families I know are missing that love factor. Wives and husbands are co-existing out of societal obligation. For the sake of their children.

Think about this: So, you've made it into marriage; what's next? Kids? Is it time to accumulate assets? Or time for you to join the women's guild at church? Ladies, I want you to think hard and deep about this. What's your end goal when it comes to marriage? Will you be satisfied as long as you earn the title of Mrs? Will your ability to have legitimate children validate you? I know that it's mainly the husband's ability to provide for his family that is placed as an integral requirement to sustain a marriage. Love has been watered down. It is not enough. However, I want to borrow from the words of Apostle Paul and say, "If he has money but does not have love, he is nothing." A little too harsh? I don't think so. It just goes to demonstrate how important love is; more so in marriage.

Go back and revisit the initial influences that led to your desire for marriage. If it doesn't align with love surrender it to God and ask Him to renew your mind so that you begin to desire marriage for the right reasons. If at this point in the book you are still asking, *what is love? Am I genuinely desiring marriage because I want to commit to love another person?* I urge you to make time to go on a love journey with God to see love through his eyes. I promise you he has all the answers to your questions. As in:

Lord, I have so many wrong reasons that dictate my desire to marry. I see it as my only way out from my poor financial status; a way out from the control of my stern father and harsh step-mum; {insert your influences}. God, you know this and you see this. Be my all in all. Right now, in this current situation. Lord, unveil your love to your daughters. Let the fullness of your love pour down on them. Open their hearts to receive it. In Jesus's Name, Amen.

I became intentional about observing the type of relationship goals set by other Christians and I will share them with you in the next section. I hope the values esteemed by other Christians will give you better insight into the values you should uphold as a believer.

#RELATIONSHIPGOALS

A hashtag followed by the words, relationship goals is trending on multiple social media platforms. It is a popular caption that usually follows a picture of a cute couple. Before I wrote this section, I decided to find content on, "Christian relationship goals" from various platforms on social media. I was truly amazed by what I discovered on there. It made me realise that there are still a lot of people out there who are seeking to engage in relationships the right way, God's way. The main relationship goal I came across was, placing God at the centre of the relationship.

The other goals included:

- Sexual purity while dating and in courtship
- Being a blessing to your spouse throughout the marriage
- Having a marriage that lasts
- Loving your spouse like Christ
- Expecting God's best
- Faithfulness
- Boyfriend/girlfriend preferable appearance, qualities and characteristics

There are people out there, like you, who are believers, single and are envisioning their future relationships. They have an idea of what they want. Most importantly, they are using the Word of God as the inspiration behind their goals. I don't think it's a coincidence that many of the quotes centre on making Christ the priority in the relationship. God has to be at the centre of it all.

I hope this will encourage you to create your own version of relationship goals by listing down your secret petitions, preferences, and expectations. Dare to jot down what you've been afraid to believe for. You don't have to look at your past experiences, do it in the name of Jesus with inspiration from the Holy Spirit. The Bible says, *"you have not because you ask not" (James 4: 2)* and furthermore, Scripture states, *"Whatever you ask for in my Name, believe and you will receive"* (John 14:13-14). There is your permit to start asking for what you want. God is literally waiting for you to ask Him, so ask. Psalm 20: 4, says, *"May he give you the desires of your heart and make all your plans succeed."* As you plan know that God is for you, waiting to give you success and grant you your heart's desires.

If you find yourself envisioning the worst-case scenario and focusing more on what would go wrong; I would encourage you to replace the awful thoughts with good ones. You would agree with me that expecting the worst actually defers your hope. So be positive and hopeful as you figure out what you would want in a relationship

VISION NOT OBSESSION

We've already established that God makes things grow (See Chapter 5). Not you, not your prayers, not a prophet, but God. For example, you may have prayed about your aspirations for marriage, talked about it with friends and sought inspiration from your ideal couples. After, doing all you could, you now have to get out of God's way and allow him to do only what he can do. You need to know that there's only so much you can do.

When you have done all you can, rest and let God. When you don't know when to stop chasing relationship matters, it stops being a journey and becomes a distraction. Therefore, persistently digging up "ideal information" of a godly relationship actually begins to feed your anxiety even more. You may have rightly been pursuing relationships as a God-given revelation but it gets out of hand when you take God's role upon yourself.

You have to discipline yourself by restricting the urge to continue working out things. The Word of God says it is for freedom that we've been made free (Galatians 5: 1). How you get to enjoy that freedom is if you don't become a slave to your own aspirations. Know when to stop. Perhaps, you've watched enough wedding videos and now it's time to delete them from your phone. That wedding board on Pinterest is good enough, you should move on to other things besides marriage that could also be beneficial to you. The manifestation of your prayer; it won't disappear if you let it go, God will make it grow.

There are things that we can't see. Farmers prepare the fields, plant seeds, and do all they can to create a conducive environment in which the seeds can grow. However, they can't force the rain to pour down, and even if they irrigate or have the knowledge of photosynthesis aiding them to manipulate the plants' growing conditions, they can't force the plant to grow. Only God can do that. We do not know the mysteries of how a tiny black seed becomes a huge red tomato. The secrets of how things grow all belong to God.

You may have exhausted every prayer you know and still feel like you fall short in your prayer requests. I would encourage you to let God. He always answers our prayers exceedingly, abundantly and above what we could ever hope for or imagine (Ephesians 3:20). Imagine if you were ignorant of God's grace that is working in your life to bringing about every good thing? You would boast in your ability to pray right? Shamelessly, taking all the credit for your answered prayer. Jesus said, ask and you will have what you asked for, and he also promised in his Word to exceed our expectations. God's blessings always outweigh our prayer requests.

When you look at what you are asking for in the present moment regarding the qualities you want in your future husband, do you realise, how nearsighted you are? You cannot tell me that you have taken into account everything that you will ever need to know for the next umpteen years ahead. However, God knows what life will be like for you ten years, even fifty years from now! As he is answering your prayer for a husband, he has taken into account all there is to consider that concerns you. So trust him to make things grow.

A DISCERNING WOMAN

The Lord told Prophet Samuel, *"People look at the outward appearance but the LORD looks at the heart" (See 1 Samuel 16:7)*. You may get caught up and place so much focus on envisioning the material things and appearance of the ideal man that you would prefer to spend the rest of your life with. Spending so much time in planning that you miss the blessings that God might have placed right in front of you. By that I mean you may miss the crucial things to look for in a man. Essentially, missing the big picture because you are too busy focusing on the things that won't necessarily matter in the long run. The intricate heart issues are the most important. Only God knows a person's heart and through the Holy Spirit reveals a persons' heart and their intentions towards you.

I cannot stress this enough, it is so easy to determine preference solely based on what your eyes can see. Just by taking one glance at a guy you can automatically disqualify him as a potential husband, thinking to yourself, "My future husband would not look like that." But I believe that it is a woman who sees a man beyond his outward appearance that is more blessed for she sees with the eyes of the Father. As children of God, we model after our Father in heaven and because he does not measure one by their physical outlook neither should we. There are women who married men who initially had nothing significant to show for and during the course of their marriage, things turned around for the better. However, as people looking into their lives from the peripheral, today we marvel at these couples as if they have always been successful. We adorn the woman as blessed to have married such a rich husband without knowing their history. There's nothing wrong with wanting a rich man or a good looking man.My desire for you is that you see beyond the lens of the natural eye and always begin by considering the heart. Don't let a certain man's appearance distract you from God's best. I believe it's going to take much more than one's appearance to sustain a marriage. You have to be open and not look down on any man. Ladies, you know what I mean. *Osanyoza*[2]. Especially, the Children of

[2] Don't demean men

God. You will agree with me that those who belong to God can change drastically from insignificant to the king in the blink of an eye. The Bible has proof of the same.

This obviously does not mean entertain any Jim and Jack that comes your way. However, as a person in Christ, it is a call to love and respect *every* man that shows an interest in you. If you should know, the Holy Spirit will teach you how to decline a relationship proposal from a man if you ought to. That's why it is also important to remain prayerful concerning these matters. You cannot be a discerning woman without prayer. Do not be given into your senses when envisioning your marital future. The key to achieving this is through cultivating your fellowship with God now as a single woman. So, when the time comes, you will be able to use your eyes of faith to identify your future spouse.

SUBMIT YOUR WAYS TO THE LORD

I hope I've inspired you to dream and state your secret petitions. It is a healthy way to figure out what you like and what is your fit. Once you outline the desires which automatically surface when you imagine your future, surrender them to God. I know how protective everyone gets over their dreams, believing that you are solely responsible for ensuring your life turns out to be perfect even to the extent that you shut God out. I know I can be stubborn. I want things to go my way. I will have it no other way. I distinctly remember when I needed to purchase a new pair of school shoes while I was still in high school and there was one particular brand that I wanted, which was popular among most of the girls at my school. My sister and I went to the shoe store and I went directly to the shelf which had the pair that I wanted. Right next to the shelf where I stood were brand new shoes which were nicer in every way than the ones I wanted, and cheaper! My sister suggested that I buy the new pair but guess what? I shut down her request. I had set my mind on purchasing the other shoes. Luckily, the pair I wanted was not available in my size and I bought the better pair instead. These shoes eventually became my favourite. I may just have narrated a typical teenage girl story to you but this experience serves as a reminder of the lengths that we will go to have our own way when God's way is better.

I've been childishly stubborn over a number of things in my life and in more times than I could ever admit the alternative has always been the best option.

I want to encourage you to be open to what God has for you rather than be locked in and get stuck on one path. God can never be wrong. God knows how to better direct your dreams, hopes, and desires. As you tell him what you are longing for with all your heart; he might just show you what he has waiting for you. Would you allow God to adjust your dreams if necessary? Some of our dreams are guided by insecurities cited by jealousy, envy, and even disappointment. How many of you describe your ideal guy based on the men you see on TV? How many of you long for your future husband to look better and be richer than your best friend's husband? You intend to use your spouse to rub it in the faces of your relatives who ever doubted that you could find a good man! Girl, I am coming for you today! When you share your longings with God, he helps you process your petitions so that they do not become a mere reaction to your problems, worries or fears.

I hope you are not worried that God will sabotage your dreams. What you want for yourself could never beat God's best for you. God has *good* plans for you which were already put in motion even before you were born. The love of God for you should give you the confidence to surrender your dreams to him. God is on your side. Allow God to have a say in your life. God will refine your dreams. He is best suited to process all your crude desires and make them all together lovely, and present them back to you well-polished and beautiful. Removing every blemish.

You need to understand that even when the vision is inspired by God, it is still possible to deter from God's initial plan for your life when you leave God out of your decision making. In your planning do not lean on your own understanding; submit your ways unto the Lord:

Lord, here are my dreams. I have my best interests at heart for my possible future. I admit I am stuck demanding only what I want and determine as suitable for my life. Renew my wrong beliefs about you. I want your will for my life. Your thoughts towards me are good. You love me. Fix my dreams where they require fixing. I confess I do not always get things right. You know better. Help me to trust you completely.

CHAPTER NINE

SOMETHING GOOD

How abundant are the good things that you have stored up for those who fear you...

Psalm 31: 19

We all have those couples that we admire and adore (#relationshipgoals). You are not prowling when you marvel at the love shared between two people. It makes sense when people observe love that is inspirational. It could be your parents, the newlyweds at your church or that Instagram couple that you follow. Love is our essence and therefore, it's not unusual when we are drawn towards it.

Every good relationship should exude love and keep getting better as the years progress. It's so easy to doubt that love could be good. But do you know that love doesn't have to be a struggle? You can actually look forward to having a wholesome marriage where you like your husband and the life you build together. I heard on the radio, the other day that one popular reason a lot of Millenials don't want to get married is that they are afraid of experiencing the ugly divorces and bad relationships like the earlier generations.

How about you? Do you think marriage will turn out to be good for you? On a certain day, Jesus was teaching his disciples, and he said, *"Which of you if his son asks for bread, will give him a stone? Or if he asks for fish, will give him a snake? If you though being evil, know how to give good gifts to your children, how much more will your father in heaven give good gifts to those who ask him?"* (See Matthew 7:11).

You have a father in heaven who gives good gifts to those who ask him. You can expect the best. If you were struggling and wondering whether it's God's will for you to have a good marriage, there is your answer. In fact, he desires to give you a great partner more than you or anyone could ever imagine! If you thought you were in the best position to identify a good partner for yourself, God can find you someone better. If you thought your friends and family know you so well that they could hook you up with someone nice, your heavenly Father can determine a more suitable man. *"Eye has not seen, ear has not heard what God has planned for those he loves"* (1 Corinthians 2:9). You are the one he loves, what your heavenly Father has planned for you is good.

FROM ABOVE

James 1:17 says, *"Every good and perfect gift comes from above.* When you are thinking about your future husband, think along those lines: good, perfect gift and, from above. *Above* is the most vital word among the four qualities, because what makes it a good and perfect gift is from whence it comes. What is from above shifts your focus from what is around you, beneath you, and inside you, to what is greater and better.

From above, it doesn't infer that this man will drop from the sky and into your life, no. Rather your focus is turned above because of the one who is there, the resurrected Jesus at the right-hand side of the Father (Colossians 3:1). The life partner you are awaiting will be from God, purposefully directed towards you. Because he is from God, your relationship will glorify Jesus. And with Jesus as the backbone of your relationship, he will also be the peace-maker when differences arise between you and your husband. When God is at the centre of your relationship all your steps will be directed by him: how you parent, your decision making, finances, careers, and worship.

PERFECT GIFT

The type of gift described here is perfect. Do you like gifts? I love gifts but only if they are what I like. Have you ever received a gift you didn't like? It becomes complex because you know the person went out of their way to get you a present and you don't want to offend them by rejecting it but at the same time, you know for sure that you will never use the gift. It's horrible!

On the other hand, when you get the PERFECT gift! It's an awesome feeling. When I get a gift that I like, I could admire it for months! If it is food, I take it in small rations; if it's wearable it becomes the clothing that is particularly well taken care of and soon enough becomes the most worn item from my wardrobe.

I know that a human being cannot be treated as a piece of clothing or food, but there are still other ways of cherishing them. It should be an exciting feeling to know that God is bringing someone your way that you will actually like, very much. You will fall in love with him, he will give you butterflies in your stomach, you will create great memories together and you will enjoy each other's company. Doesn't that make you feel good?

I like that this Holy Spirit inspired Scripture uses the word, "perfect". We always seem to run away from that word. But here God's says "perfect" and so you should set the hope bar so high my friend because perfect means perfect.

A gift is perfect according to the individual. What's perfect for me can't be what's perfect for you. At the moment, my perfect gift would be a Golden State Warrior's jersey, specifically, number 30. That probably means nothing to you, you may want as a gift, your choice of make-up or a mac book. I may try and guess but you are in a better position to know what you would want. Since God knows what your perfect gift would be, he will give you a tailor-made preference.

In addition, a gift is not earned. It comes freely. I know we are in an era where people announce their birthdays as soon as we reach their birthday month, to ensure people remember and, get presents or plan something for them. I guess I prefer the old school way, I like people to remember on their own and get me presents, willingly. I believe those are the best gifts because it indicates that they had me on their mind and I didn't have to do anything to force their hand. God gives us gifts because he has us on his mind and knows exactly what would make us happy. Gifts are a delight and they come freely. If you earn it then it's no longer a gift, it's more like a wage— a payment for your efforts. Gifts are simply meant to be received with gratitude and gladness. May you see the partner God gives you as a gift. I pray, that you do not try to earn love by using your own efforts.

GOOD

God looked at all that he had made and said it was very good (see Genesis 1:31). All that God has made is without fault, nothing needs fixing. All his works are marvellous. God pays attention to every detail and pours love and effort into all his work making it very good. One distinct characteristic of anything good is that it does not bring you harm. This is a very important quality that you should seek out in a relationship. Love is not supposed to hurt. Love shouldn't make you sick and afraid. Love shouldn't make you worry. The gift of relationship that God gives to his children is good.

Now I know you are familiar with Proverbs 18:22 that says. *"He who finds a wife finds what is good and receives favour from the Lord."* God endorses the union of marriage as a blessing. When you imagine your marriage understand that it will be good all around, you will both be good for and to each other. It will be a relationship that adds value to both your lives. Your union will be an excellent work of the Lord.

I know you maybe be wondering, what if it's not good? I don't want to raise my hopes up just to be disappointed. I want to remind you again, that we live by faith and not by sight (2 Corinthians 5:7). Dare to trust God's Word, he will never let you down. Christian couples may disappoint you, the older couples in your family may disappoint you, and young couples you look up to may fall short. God is not asking you to pretend as if you haven't or won't experience all of that, he wants you to place more confidence in His Word.

TOO GOOD TO BE TRUE

A lot of women have been conditioned to expect the worst when it comes to marriage. Consider the women who've attempted to escape abusive marriages but were advised that, "Banja ndikupilira.[3]" and imagine young women with marriage aspirations who have witnessed the horrible outcomes as a result of this common advice. It's a scary thought to know that you won't be spared from this counsel when you decide to get married.

Society has conditioned women to expect harsh treatment from their future husbands and subconsciously prepare for it. Most women cultivate defensive mechanisms in advance to ensure they are ready to strike back when the time comes. While in conversation about relationships with a friend, one of us said, "I will make sure that I have my own money so that in the event that my husband cheats on me, I would leave." At that moment it dawned on me that our words were a reflection of what we'd subconsciously been believing. Such sentiments expose your beliefs about the nature of relationships. It is accepting that it is almost inevitable that you will encounter adultery in your marriage. Another popular hypothetical phrase shared among unmarried women is, "I won't let his mother boss me around." Again, is it reflects that you've accepted the stereotypical belief that you will have an overbearing woman for a mother-in-law. Here is a thought: does God want you to live life perpetually expecting the worst? You don't need to be a wife first to know that, marriage is not supposed to be a lifetime of painful endurance. Marriage is not a constant burden that God expects every spouse to carry the rest of their lives. Sometimes it's as if drama gives life to relationships when as a matter of fact it's only the devil doing what he knows best: stealing, killing and destroying. You may feel justified to expect the worst based on past relationships.You tell yourself, you are just being honest. But I believe, marriage is a blessing and when God blesses, he adds no sorrow to it[1].

---

[3] The key to making a marriage work is endurance

A good marriage is worth believing. Before I deliberately sought God on my desires for marriage, my expectations were also horrible. We truly need to shift our perspective of marriage by embracing God's heart for us. A lot of unmarried women would agree with me that they've found themselves in a position where they, undoubtedly desire marriage but fear the outcome. I'd heard people say that once you are married, you become unlovable to your husband. A lot has been said that snuffs out hope.

Jesus demonstrated a Christ-like love and expects godly marriages to emulate this type of love. A sacrificial love that nourishes, cherishes and respects[2]. Stand firm on God's Word in Psalms 84:11 (KJV), *"... the LORD will give grace and glory: No good thing will he withhold from those who walk uprightly."* As His children walking in His ways, you can confidently believe that God intends for your future marriage to be good. Marriage ought to last for a lifetime and I believe, it should be enjoyed within its longevity. May you get out of marriage what God designed for it, knowing full well that his plans for us are good (Jeremiah 29:11). The world may call you overly optimistic but strive to believe for a good marriage.

It may feel like it's too good to be true. Like can we keep it up as our years in marriage advance? I believe the answers to those questions is, yes. God who is good and true will coexist in your marriage. God is behind every act of goodness that happens in your life and as long as he is a part of your marriage you will encounter his goodness.

At the end of the day, it is God who makes marriage unique for believers. For you have chosen to embrace His ways and let him take centre stage in your life. Remember this truth, *"Not once have I seen the righteous forsaken"* (Psalm 37:25). Whenever you are fretful of encountering constant disappointment in your future marriage, remember God's promises to you.

GOD IS GOOD

If you walk into any African church you will hear the saints declaring in unison that, "God is good all the time, all the time God is good!" We need to be constantly reminded that God is good. The Bible says, "Jesus went around doing good,"[3] I've encountered good people whose joy and peace was infectious and thought to myself how are you always so nice? It's a blessing to meet people who have a big heart. They always have room to serve and love others. Yet, even these nice people may lose their cool sometimes. But, God remains good. This is such a deep truth that we all need to internalise. God will never stop being and doing good. Even on account that you miss the mark, God will continue to be good. In the same way, God is love, he is also good—goodness stems out of his nature.

The following verse is a personal favourite on God's goodness, mercy, and loving-kindness: Titus 3:4-5 reads: *But when the goodness and loving kindness of God our savior appeared, he saved us, not because of works done by us in righteousness, but according to his own mercy..."* This verse grips me every time. It serves as a reminder that apart from Jesus, we are not deserving of any good thing.

As you are believing and praying for a partner I want you to acknowledge that a good marriage is a result of the goodness, loving-kindness, and mercy of God. You are not entitled to or deserving of a good marriage. It's because and only because of Jesus that you will taste the goodness of marriage. It's not because of anything you have done. A good marriage is not a reward for your prayer, purity, dedication or good looks. I recently shared with someone that exercising purity does not exempt you from meeting an awful guy. You can pray, hope and, "do all the right things" as a single woman but meeting a good man and being in a good marriage all comes down to God's mercy. And the beautiful thing is his goodness and mercy is working in your life[4].

I want to help you avoid making the mistake of believing that *you* make the beautiful marriage happen. You should have an eternal dependence on the goodness of God and not on your own efforts. It will be by this same grace that you will work hard to make your marriage work[5]. Like for any relationship, you will have to draw strength from God to make your marriage work. A good marriage is both built up and sustained by grace.

CHAPTER TEN

FLOCKING TOGETHER

Where you go I will go, and where you stay I will stay. Your people will be my people and your God my God.

Ruth 1:16

Friends play an integral role in our lives. Everyone wants someone who accepts them for who they are, no matter how indifferent they may be. It is beautiful to be around other people who have similar interests as you. Getting to share life with other people is a grand blessing and a privilege. Somehow, friends make everything better. In a world filled with diverse people; when you find your "tribe," you keep them close.

I discovered my "tribe" in other ladies who believed in dating with intention and living in purity. For a long time, I had internalised everything I believed about abstinence and having meaningful relationships. It was a lonely path. Knowing that there were others like me, freed me and affirmed the beliefs I held about relationships.

I used to feel like I was exaggerating when I didn't want to date "just for fun." The people around me disagreed with my point of view; they accused me of displaying a, "holier than thou" attitude. I had friends who were worried about me for not being open to dating during that period. They didn't understand when I told them it was God's desire that I guard my heart. Convinced that I was on the right path, I persevered alone but not having a support system made it difficult.

My main prayer was for God to give me friends who were on the same journey. God answered my prayer and he brought women into my life who were pursuing him. These are women from all walks of life with one goal: to live guided by their faith in Jesus Christ. Together, we share knowledge and valuable lessons that we are learning through our individual journeys. I am truly blessed to have friends who understand me and with whom I can be vulnerable.

CHOOSE WISELY

One crucial adjustment I had to make after I had given my life to Christ was to change friends. I had resolved in my heart that I would no longer live frivolously. I knew that the friends I previously had would not help me grow into the woman God wanted me to become. I had to choose to leave the life that was led by self-gratification and that I perceived as fun, for a life that was guided by purpose and the peace of God.

Friends have the power to influence your decisions and way of life. It doesn't matter your age, friends will always have a major influence on you. It is vital that you choose them wisely. Friends are to be chosen. You need to intentionally surround yourself with people who understand your purpose in life. Those who will build you up, edify you and help you draw closer to Jesus. Friends with whom you can be vulnerable and those who can guard your secrets and keep them confidential. And most of all, you need a friend who will be your prayer partner always ready to pray with you and for you.

You need to identify friends who you can trust, especially with the area of your love life. The topic of relationships is a tricky one. It can be very uncomfortable to talk about relationships with another person. To honestly express yourself to another individual is not easy. That is why you need to surround yourself with friends who are trustworthy. Someone who will not ridicule you. You could openly share with them deep and sensitive issues. You have a good friend in the person who won't mock you for admitting that you desire to get married. There are other friends who say the meanest things to each other. This one is a popular one, "you don't even have a boyfriend, why would you of all people be thinking about marriage." I've heard friends say to each other, *"Asisi inuyo mwakula, musamaganizenso zabanja mungopangazoti mukhale ndimwana basi."*[4]

There are friends who endorse premarital sex and ridicule those practicing abstinence. Check your friends who slap the hope out of you for esteeming faithfulness in a relationship. Those who present to you a distorted view of marriage. You cannot flourish in those kinds of friendships, they will only diminish your hope for a godly marriage.

I've held on to the beautiful reminder that God listens in on our conversations.[1] And I believe he is proud when we treat each other kindly. Friendships should be endowed with kindness. Friends who are catty and jealous won't edify you. Friends who have a good character bring peace into their friendships. You shouldn't have friends who stress you out and are constantly causing drama. Friendships should be healthy and peaceful. Avoid toxic relationships at all costs. In a world of shady and insensitive comments directed towards unmarried women. Kindness would go a long way.

I know sometimes, what explains our friends' behaviours are the hurts and negative experiences which have left them scarred and as a result contributes to their tainted beliefs and expectations about relationships and marriage. That's why it's equally important to use the Word of God to filter sentiments relayed in your conversations. Ultimately, it is wise to have more friends who base what they say on the Word of God. Those who are Spirit-led and not carnal (Romans 8:6). Surround yourself with great women and men of God who will take you to greater heights in your faith and life.

---

[4] Sister, you are now grown up, don't even think about marriage anymore, just have a child.

THE SAME MISSION

In this section, I want to highlight the characteristics of a friendship with a person who is Spirit-led and purpose-oriented. You should know in advance, this group of friends sets the friendship bar extremely high. This group of friends were young, living in an immoral environment and far away from home.

Daniel, Hananiah, Mishael, and Azariah were among young men who were taken from Jerusalem when it was besieged by King Nebuchadnezzar of Babylon. These four boys qualified as ideal men to enter the king's service. They were taken in by the chief of the king's court officials and were expected to learn the literature and language of the Babylonians. The king assigned them a daily amount of food and wine from his table. They were to be trained for three years, and after that, they would enter the king's service. (See Daniel 1: 1-5).

However, Daniel had resolved that he would not defile himself with the Babylonian royal food and wine, so he asked the chief official for permission not to eat the food nor drink the wine. Fortunately for Daniel, God had caused the chief official to show favour and sympathy to him. Nonetheless, the chief official fearing for his life still denied Daniel's request. Determined to stay true to his God, Daniel convinced the guard appointed over him and his three friends to test the alternative diet on them for ten days. The guard would also observe their appearance in comparison to the other young men who ate from the king's table and then to decide the way forward based on the outcome that he would see. The diet included only vegetables and water as food and drink. At the end of the ten days, Daniel and his friends looked better nourished and healthier than any of the other young men eating the royal food. So the guard took away the king's choice food and wine and gave them vegetables instead (see Daniel 1: 8-16). God gave these four young men knowledge and understanding of every kind of literature and learning. At the end of the training, the chief official presented these four young men to the king. The king talked with them and was greatly impressed by Daniel, Hananiah, Mishael, and Azariah, so they entered the king's service.

FRIENDSHIP SECRETS FROM THE FOUR MEN

i.GOD CENTERED

Right from the beginning, Daniel made a resolution that he would not eat the food or take the wine from the king's table because he didn't want to defile his God. Anyone would consider it fortunate to eat from the king's table but Daniel and his friends viewed it differently, because the Babylonian king did not believe in God, and Babylonians were known for pagan worship. As a result, Daniel and his friends feared that they might eat food that had been consecrated to idols[2]. That is why Daniel referred to him partaking of the food from the king's table as defilement because the law clearly spoke against idol worship (Exodus 34:14). The Bible has no record of his friends objecting to Daniel's proposal and this shows that they were all in it together. They put God first, even if it meant forfeiting all those privileges.

WHY IS IT IMPORTANT TO HAVE FRIENDS WHO PUT GOD FIRST?

When you have friends who dedicate their lives to pleasing God, you are assured that you hold common values based on the Word of God. These values would then guide your friendship and help you make better life choices. This differs from having friends who are carnal-minded and who could easily weigh you down. They are the type who will give you advice that they believe is rational but falls short according to God's standard.

Friends who follow Jesus add value to your life. It's common in most households that behaviour change is attributed to friends when a child becomes rebellious in the home. And it's usually true. In the same way, if you associate with friends who possess commendable qualities, their good habits will also rub off on you.

Sometimes there are things that we keep from telling even our family members but could tell a friend. Consider Daniel and his friends who were far from home and with no known parents or older guardians; yet as friends they were able to make an informed decision based on their mutual relationship with God. It's in moments like those that the counsel from Spirit-led friends matters the most. I recall an experience where counsel from my Jesus-loving friends superseded the advice I was getting from other people that I also respected. I was told by other friends and relatives to make sure that I was dating by my senior year of college to ensure that I had a boyfriend who I would later marry once I graduated. They believed if I wasn't dating by that set time, I would experience difficulties in finding a life partner, later on. The common expectation is that the next step after college is to get married. The assumption is that if you don't have a boyfriend by the time you finish college there is little chance that you will get married in the future. It may seem absurd to some, as it did to me, but that was before I realised how many people adhere to this. It has become an acceptable norm. This is for sure sensible advice. They were looking out for me, I know and making sure that I wouldn't die alone. But as a child of God you know there are a lot of loopholes there, the major one being taking matters into your own hands and leaving God out. At this time I leaned hard on friends who had graduated without being in a relationship in their senior years of college and they provided the spiritual and moral support I needed. It is truly a blessing to have friends who will remind you that God orders your steps and you don't have to rush anything.

ii.IN ONE ACCORD

The story narrated above conveys that the four men rejected the food and wine from the king's table and chose to eat only vegetables and take water as their beverage, *together*. In other events that unfolded while they were in Babylon, the four men had to pray together at Daniel's request after their lives were threatened when the king commanded the execution of all wise men including Daniel and his friends (Daniel 2: 17-18). In another incident, Shadrach, Meshach, and Abednego refused to bow down to an image of gold that was set up by King Nebuchadnezzar, and for that reason were thrown into a fiery furnace (Daniel 3:1323).

You can clearly see that these friends were each other's support system. They were able to work together and help each other because they were united towards the same goal. There wasn't one doubting friend. They were in one accord in their faith and always supported each other through prayer. From the time they were young, they found themselves in extreme and difficult situations. Their faith was tested over and over again but they always stood their ground, *together*.

You need friends who esteem the power of prayer and who will pray with you especially in times when you are in dire need. You can't ask just any friend to pray for you no matter how good of a friend they are. Friends who have a relationship with God are the ones who are better equipped to pray. Friends who you can be open to. Friends who are always ready to pray with you in every situation. Those are the real friends who you can celebrate good times with because they understand your journey.

Have friends who will keep you accountable. These friends would particularly be valuable when you make the decision to remain sexually pure until you are married. They would encourage you, give you honest advice and also rebuke you if you deter from your path. While pursuing similar goals, you could share the highs and lows experienced along your journey. Imagine how many contradicting views you would receive from a friend who holds different values? You would probably always come out confused from conversations with that person. Or you might end up compromising by resorting to "agree to disagree" on the matter. Both options are unhealthy in comparison to having a friend with whom you share similar beliefs, for at the core of your friendship is your mutual relationship with Jesus.

iii.YOU RISE, I RISE

Good friends have your best interests at heart. When Daniel was promoted to a high position, he put in a good word for his friends and they were also offered better posts (Daniel 2: 48-49). You can trust true friends to genuinely celebrate with you when something good happens. They would not sport envy or jealousy. It is not okay, to have a friend who is jealous, selfish or one with narcissist tendencies. They could never be a good friend to you; you have to let them go.

As you share your journey of singleness with friends who are also single; it is inevitable that one of you will get into a relationship before the other. If you were to get a boyfriend before your friend, a good friend would genuinely be happy for you. A good friend will steer you in the right direction. A good friend will do for you what they would do for themselves. They will wish for you what they would want for themselves. A good friend wouldn't be envious towards you because they know that there is an abundance of goodness in God's storehouse; more than enough for the both of you.

BE A GOOD FRIEND

The title of this section sounds like the usual advice mums give to their little children. However, I believe that this is exceptional advice that is useful for all age groups. It's easy for you to list down the qualities you expect your friends to have and forget that you also have a role to play in the friendship.

The person that comes to my mind with tremendous friendship qualities is Ruth. The name Ruth means *a friend*[3] and Ruth was indeed an extraordinary friend. She was a woman who was selfless, humble, loving and kind. The story of Ruth is found in a book in the Bible of the same name. Ruth was a daughter-in-law to Naomi. Naomi was a widow living with two sons in a foreign country called Moab. Naomi and her family had left their home, Bethlehem in Judah, searching for greener pastures to escape the famine that was in the country. Naomi's husband died while they were in the land of Moab and she was left with her two sons. Her two sons married Moabite women, Ruth and Orpah. However, after living for ten years in Moab, Naomi's two sons also died, leaving Orpah and Ruth as widows.

Naomi decided to return home after she heard that God had delivered Bethlehem from the famine. She started off to Bethlehem with her daughters-in-law but during the course of the journey, she decided to send them back home, to Moab. At first, Ruth and Orpah both refused to go back but after persistent pleading from Naomi, Orpah returned home. But Ruth maintained her disposition and chose to stay with Naomi.

The return to Bethlehem did not make life better for Naomi and Ruth. As widows, they had no husbands to provide for them. You can tell by the remarks made by Naomi to her daughter's in-law, that it was of grave importance for a woman to have a husband at this time (See Ruth 1:11-

13; 3: 1). On their own the women were poor. As a result, given that they arrived in Bethlehem at a time of the barley harvest, Ruth opted to work in the fields and collect leftovers from the harvesters.

Ruth was compassionate towards her mother-in-law, Naomi in ways beyond what was expected of her. Such friendships run deep and can help you get through the hard times. Ruth has already demonstrated that friendships go deeper than casual reactions. To Naomi, Ruth was the friend that became family. Given that they were related as in-laws, she had the right to leave Naomi after her husband had died. Ruth was not liable to stay or even maintain a relationship with Naomi (you've probably heard the stereotypical stories of mothers-in-law). However, Ruth demonstrated a better way. She was the strong, God-loving woman who rallied behind her friend at a difficult time. Absolutely irreplaceable! What a gift!

Boaz, one of the richest men in Bethlehem (as it so happens it was Boaz's field where Ruth was gleaning barley) said of Ruth, *"I've been told about all you have done for your mother-in-law since the death of your husband; how you left your father and mother and your home land and came to live with a people that you did not know before"* (Ruth 11:2). After saying this, Boaz went on to bless Ruth for what she had done for her mother-in-law (See Ruth 11:3-4). In another instance, he also told her that: *"All my townsmen know that you are a woman of noble character"* (Ruth 3: 11b)—she also got the attention of prominent men in this village for her kindness. I pray people talk about your kind-heartedness

Be the friend that lends a listening ear to someone struggling in the wait. Be there for them, ready to offer them a hug and to speak life-giving words. Always praying over them and loving on them. Be the friend who doesn't judge, however, tempted you may be. If I could choose two things to do for a friend struggling in the wait, it would be to listen and pray. As people, we don't always fully understand another person's experiences. So when someone shares with you their struggles, you don't have to give in your two cents all the time. The beauty of listening is that it gives you the chance to process the conversation and to pray silently to a God who is able to comfort and release his love over every situation.

It's clear in the story of Ruth that her noble character didn't go unnoticed by God. She, a Moabitess, became a part of the genealogy of Jesus himself![4] God surely takes friendships seriously. The selflessness and kindness of Ruth's actions which were purely out of love earned her great honour. She was only being a good daughter-in-law and trying to survive, but her works did not go unnoticed; the whole town and its prominent men observed her actions. Being a good friend should not be taken lightly. It is an act that pleases man, and most importantly, it pleases God.

BE YOUR OWN FRIEND

We have deduced what it means to be a good friend. Among other things, a good friend is kind, a reliable confidant, your support system and most of all a lover of God. The first step to becoming a friend to yourself is to treat yourself like you would treat your best friend. The person who you spend the most time with is yourself. Before you extend kindness to others, you should first be kind to yourself.

Being your own friend becomes especially important when you feel down. On the days you are hurting, you will have to show yourself extra compassion and kindness. You might even go further to build yourself up in your faith. The Bible says of David that he encouraged himself in the Lord (1 Samuel 30:6 KJV). When you read several of the Psalms written by David, you will note that he would speak to himself. In Psalm 43: 5, he said, *"Why are you downcast, O my soul? Why are you disturbed within me? Put your hope in the Lord, for I will yet praise him, my savior and my God."* This excerpt of the Psalmist speaking to himself, narrated in the second person could pass off as a conversation occurring between two friends. This behaviour is not strange, there is a psychological term for it called, self-talk. Self-talk[5] is an internal monologue that is done out loud or silently. Self-talk can either be negative or positive.

As a believer, sometimes you may have faith in your spirit but the soul, with its fickle emotions, gets in the way and resists your faith. You know the things you say to yourself like, "Who would ever love someone like you"... "You will probably die alone." You can put a stop to this deplorable self-talk by choosing to stand firm in your faith and align yourself with God's truth. You can say to yourself, "I am accepted in the beloved"... "the Lord will never leave nor forsake me." Ultimately, be your own cheerleader and encourager guided by the Holy Spirit and God's Word.

FRIENDS OF GOD

Jesus is the personification of a friend who is closer than a brother. Remember, Jesus, in reference to himself said, *"Great love is this, that one lay down his life for his friends"* (John 15:13, See Chapter 1). Jesus extended friendship towards us by showering us with love when we were undeserving. When we didn't consider him a friend, Jesus gave up his life for us. You should cherish your friendship with him.

As your friend, he is concerned about the affairs of your life including your love life. He cares about you and he is always ready to help. His arms are open wide when you need an embrace, and he is the shoulder that you can lean on. He is your intercessor. In addition, Jesus sent one like him, the Holy Spirit, who is a counsellor, advocate, and guide. As a child of God, the Holy Spirit lives in you. He is always present with you. Take advantage of his presence and tap into this power. The Holy Spirit is the power of God that gives us the ability to trust the promises of God and on the days when you are your own worst enemy, he will enable you to be gracious towards yourself. Be conscious of the Holy Spirit. Make him your best friend. Share with him your deep concerns and your struggles. Before, you post your successes on social media, celebrate them with him. Utilise the moments you feel lonely to be alone with him; you will discover new things about yourself that you wouldn't have known otherwise. Sometimes, we live by reacting to whatever life throws at us. As you constantly fellowship with the Holy Spirit, you will get to know the, "real you" that has been unable to fully flourish inhibited by the struggles in the wait. The next time you need support from a friend, I encourage you to tap into the power of Spirit of God which has been made available to you.

Even on the days when you don't feel him near, God is still with you. He is the friend that sticks closer than a brother, always looking out for you. Know that God always hears you and he will always be there for you.

IRON SHARPENS IRON

The phrase, "Iron sharpens iron," is found in Proverbs 27:17: "As Iron sharpens iron, so one person sharpens another." There are two points we can make from this proverb. The first being that as people we need to constantly be in fellowship with each other. Another thing that I want to explore in the rest of the section is the analogy of iron sharpening iron in reference to encouraging each other in the Lord and keeping each other accountable. If an iron cast tool is blunt, it becomes ineffective and less useful. This suggests that it is possible that a friend could fall short and would require another friend to help them get back on their feet. One way we can grow and make each other better in friendships is by always being honest with each other.

There will be moments when you need to have the "awkward" talks with your friends, when you have done, or your friend has done something that's off the mark and you need to talk it out. Sometimes we are unaware of our own flaws and become stubborn when someone points out our error. Yet, it's in those moments—when you don't want to hear it that true friends will still be honest with you. It is true that those who flatter you, lay a trap at your feet (Proverbs 29:5). It doesn't feel good to be corrected since everyone likes to be right. However, be open to correction. The initial reaction, for example, if your friend said you were leading a guy on, would be to deny it and argue your case. But instead of getting defensive, it's wiser to pause and reflect on what your friend has said. Friends who tell you the truth have your best interests at heart. Learn to be open to what they have to say.

If you are like me, it becomes difficult when the tables turn and you have to confront a friend. So I usually resort to praying about it first and I would advise you to do the same. Your goal should be to speak to your friend in a loving and kind manner, removing any sort of emphasis or exaggeration, and also choosing to be mindful of how sensitive they may be to what you have to tell them. Avoid turning the matter into a quarrel. If you notice that in the midst of the conversation, there is the chance of the issue getting out of hand, let it go. Pointing out errors and becoming involved in another person's love life is awkward, no one wants to appear as if they are better than their friend. I believe that where feelings are involved things get complicated and you won't always understand the complex issues happening in someone else's love life so always handle such matters with utmost care.

CHAPTER ELEVEN

WITH LOVE, FROM YOUR SISTERS IN CHRIST

There are a lot of single women like you who have chosen God's way of pursuing marriage and relationships. I asked a few friends whom I trust to offer advice and honestly share with you, their experiences as single women with an emphasis on their struggles, their expectations and the role of faith throughout their journey. We honoured the privacy of some by keeping their names anonymous. The following are their open letters to you.

TRUST IN GOD'S PLAN FOR YOUR LIFE

Dear sister in Christ,

I don't know what season of life this letter finds you in, but let me start by saying that you are dearly loved by God. Above your desires and your goals, there is a Creator who has made you for himself; he calls you precious and he has tattooed your name on the palm of his hand. He is enough for you ☺ Christ is in you; you are complete. May you walk in the light of that truth all the days of your life (may we all).

As you wait on God and trust Him in the area of your love life, know that you are not alone. In practice, the plan of God for you is good and therefore, enjoy this season of singlehood knowing that it's not going to last forever. Turn to the Holy Spirit for help on the hard days (turn to

Him even on the easy ones). And if there are moments when the promise seems to tarry, anchor yourself in the truth of God's Word.

I pray that God is writing the sort of story that one day when you meet your future husband, you will say that he was worth the wait.

With love from,

Elita

I LEARNT THE HARD WAY

Dear Sister,

I think it's only right that I start this letter by giving you a picture of what my "love life" in my twenties has looked like so far. At the beginning of my twenties, I found myself consecutively getting entangled with two guys that were not saved. Both relationships ended badly and after the second relationship ended, I felt I needed to make some changes to ensure that I never found myself in such a situation again. So I decided to do a 2-year "man fast". I intentionally stayed far away from "love interests" and made time to pray for this area of my life and to learn what godly men and godly relationships ought to look like. After my fast ended, an amazing God-fearing man came knocking on my door and said he wanted to take me out on a date. I did not see it coming at all. As much as my man fast was over, I just didn't think I would get into a relationship anytime soon. After much prayer and counsel from older men and women that I respect, I decided that I would accept his invitation and go on this date. A few dates later, we went ahead and made the decision to officially start courting. And as I write this letter, we have been together for 6 months and by the grace of God, I am enjoying this process of falling in love with him.

When Antonia approached me to write a letter to single Christian girls, I asked myself what I wish I had known before I got into this relationship. A lot of things come to mind but I'll share just one with you: I wish I had known that singlehood is not exclusively preparation for courtship and marriage. I spent my man fast learning what a godly man and a godly woman ought to look like for the purpose of knowing what to look for in a husband and how to one day be a good wife. I wish that hadn't been the initial reason behind it. I wish I had learnt what a godly woman ought to look like for the purpose of being the woman that God desires I be. For a long time, I thought singlehood was a phase of life that I was just passing through until I was ready to get married. The dangerous thing there was that I looked at marriage as the be all and end all of life. But it's not- **God is!** Marriage won't complete me- **God does!** I know this now, but I wish I had known this earlier so that I didn't put so much pressure on my singlehood to prepare me for marriage. I wish I had pursued God just for the sake of knowing Him more. Don't get me wrong, it's so important to learn about godly relationships while we're single but I just think you ought to have the right motives.

I'd like to share another thing with you. This one is something I'm glad I knew before I got into this relationship: I'm glad I knew that guys who were not saved were a no-go zone. I learnt this the hard way. Like I said earlier, I got into two different relationships with guys that weren't saved and that didn't go well. As much as the guys were different, both relationships caused me to compromise and then regret. When God tells us not to be unequally yoked with nonbelievers, he tells us because he is a loving father that knows what is best for us. My sisters, I beg of you, if he is not saved, stay away from him! He might be super nice and super sweet, heck he might be nicer and sweeter than the Christian guys that you know. However, if that sweetness and niceness do not come from Jesus, it's extremely likely that it'll go away one day and be replaced with something nasty and sour. Wouldn't you rather be single than joined to someone nasty and sour? Plus, if you are saved, then your relationship with Jesus is by far the most important thing in your life. Wouldn't you want to share this with the person you're doing life with? I repeat: My sisters, I beg of you, if he is not saved, stay away from him!

As I end this letter, I just want to tell you that God is more interested in your love life than you are. Pursue Him, and trust His plan for you.

Much much love,

Your sister in Christ

RUN YOUR COURSE

Dear loves,

I've heard people say of their spouses, "they complete me", "they are my better half" and it does not sit well with my spirit. Dear lady expecting marriage, I want you to constantly be conscious that you are a whole person now. Nothing missing, nothing lacking and nothing broken. You are complete in Christ Jesus (Colossian 1:10). A spouse can't complete a person. A spouse is a person to share your life with, not a half. Your completion is in Him, not him. I love that, two people in their own wonderfulness can get together and complement each other as they build their marriage. I think that's when "One can put 1000 to flight and two can put 10000 to flight" [1]comes into reality. Refuse to neglect ownership of your personhood by hiding, even behind your connection with your future spouse.

Have you ever sat down and considered how we do not really get to make many of our own life-altering decisions? Very few things in life are actually your choice. Or a result of your making. Do you doubt this? Here are instances for you to consider: on average the schools you went to were never your choice. At most, they were selected for you. For some even the subjects you studied there were chosen for you. The job you'll have is dictated by the economy and available job opportunities. Where you live right now might also not have been your choice. We don't pick our parents, our siblings or even our children.

However, God gives us the massive choice of picking who we want to spend our lives with. This thought excites me all the time. I believe getting into a relationship as well as staying in one is largely a consequence of choices and decisions. It is such an honour to get to choose who can and who cannot enter into our lives. It is also empowering to know that God trusts me to make the right decisions with regard to whom I would like to build my legacy.

You also get to choose what kind of spouse you are going to be for your future husband. The investments that you make in the Word of God in your season of singleness are what will determine what kind of building materials you will bring to your marriage. So my dear lady, know that you can remain calm and there is no pressure. Sow the Word of God into your spirit. No dating tips or relationship seminars will suffice. Let the His Word and the Holy Spirit guide you to make wise and correct decisions regarding who and when you will marry.

I came across a quote the other day which said, "If God can find Adam a wife when he's the only human being in the world, He can get you, somebody". Wow, what a thought. In a world where there is so much information on how to find "the one" and relationship tips for Christian singles, it is comforting to ponder upon such truth. Dear single lady whatsoever concerns you, also concerns Papa God. He is deeply concerned about who you marry. So my love, relax. Rest in Him. It will happen, at the right time and with the right person. I would suggest that you get busy serving the Lord. I like to tell myself ever so often that as a child of God, I have a course to run. And I want above all things that my future husband should find me running my course.

Love,
Your Sis in Christ.

EVERLASTING LOVE

My dear, wonderful sisters,

I'm going to start off this letter by citing one of my favourite Bible verses; Jeremiah 31:3:

"The LORD hath appeared of old unto me, saying, Yea, I have loved thee with an everlasting love: therefore with loving kindness have I drawn thee."

An everlasting love: that's perfection itself. It doesn't come from people, from money, from fame. An everlasting love; that's God Himself. And that's what I want you to hold on to, whether you are single or married.

When I was thinking about what to say to you, Antonia made this suggestion: "Be honest and imagine that you are talking to a single version of yourself. But at the same time, you are addressing some of the challenges you've witnessed other single women face."

So (drumroll!) here goes:

I'll bet most of you think of getting married in your late twenties, or maybe early thirties. But we never really know what plans God has in store for us. As I'm writing this I will be turning forty-three. I got married on 12th November 2016, four days after my 41st birthday. You can imagine some of the challenges I had faced from society over the years. I'll just list a few:

Well-meaning people contacted "prophets" who told them that I had been bewitched from birth, and would therefore never get married.

Level-headed people told me to forget about ever getting married and just look for someone with whom I could get a child (yes, that was the expression which was used; "get" a child).

Others felt I had brought my singleness on myself; I should have used more make-up, worn better clothes, invested in grooming.

Still, others said that I was too focused on my school and career, again, I had "brought this" on myself.

And then there were the match-makers. To my knowledge, at least two men were advised to contact me on the understanding that marriage would be a foregone conclusion. At least if people tell you they are setting you up, that's different. But I'm talking about a man calling me, acting like we were already together, and getting annoyed at the fact that I was surprised by it all.

And then there were those who asked me if I had a family, and they weren't referring to my parents or siblings.

I wish I could tell you that I reacted gracefully to all these scenarios, as well as those I haven't mentioned because of time and space. But no, I felt frustrated and annoyed by the assumptions.

I should also say that there were moments of self-doubt; I kept wondering why, after "negotiating" with God many times through prayer and giving Him a list of requirements, the right man was not coming along. So what I'm saying is that sometimes our negative attitudes about singleness come from what other people are saying, but at other times they come from within (I'm reminded here, of a line from the hymn *O Jesus I have Promised*: "My foes are ever near me, around me and *within*". But I also had good friends who understood and a great sister. And what I would say is, through all the years, even when things seemed shaky, it was a belief that God is always in control that kept me going, as well as cultivating a sense of humour.

One of the lessons I have learnt, and continue to learn, is that every day is precious. What this means is that marriage is not the end of the journey; it is a continuing step in the journey. And because every day is precious, God uses it to continue shaping us into who He wants us to be.

He loves us, not because we know how to groom ourselves, or because we smile a lot (both are good things, by the way ☺). He loves us because He is love. He considers us unique. Don't ever forget that. So embrace those gifts that He has given you. They are gifts that you are going to draw from in your life. I'll give you an example; I have always loved writing. When I got married, I realized one day that I wasn't writing anymore. It wasn't as if my husband had stopped me; I had just stopped. And I realized that I had let go of a beautiful gift. I've slowly started getting it back; it was something that I had been blessed with, and I now know I should not cast it aside. I took it for granted when I was single. What treasures has He given you that you haven't focused on?

I'll repeat; He has loved us with an everlasting love. The single woman who remembers this will walk tall, knowing that in God's sight she is perfect, she is special, and she is blessed. The married woman who remembers this will walk tall, too, knowing that in God's sight she is perfect, she is special, she is blessed. So what I'm saying is, single or married, the greatest gift you can claim for yourself is a focus on

God's everlasting love.

You are learning, and so am I, because life continues to be a journey.

Stay blessed,

Timwa Lipenga

OPEN SPACES

Dear Perfectionist,

There is grace to let you forgive yourself.

I have struggled with what to write for this entry and I was just going to ask Antonia to pick some pages from my journals and write those here. Because I will admit, I sometimes look back to my journals and I think, "How was this written by the same person reading this? The writer is so wise, so insightful and totally saw a lot of things coming. You should have stuck to what past you was saying, present you, she definitely had her eye on the ball."

But I will just share on where I am today. I was having dinner with a friend a few days ago and the subject moved to the number of times we had been bridesmaids and why we weren't *actively* moving towards marriage. I will share only one thing to avoid writing an entire book as well.

Freedom.

My friend and I realized we liked "the freedom to do what we liked." On family, it was big enough that you had expectations required of you; you share chores and you ask, "What is personal space?" when people from small families speak of it. In general, you tend to act in the knowledge that there are others who will be directly affected by your actions.

We had earlier curfews than our brothers, we were scolded for being seen walking around with a boy even though we weren't "actually doing anything," we were forbidden from having a boyfriend for most of the years that mattered and no one came to say that it was finally okay to be in a relationship when suddenly marriage was expected of us.

Living with people in boarding schools and college, having to share space, we recognized that we were fine in that area. We know how to live with people and move towards goals for the betterment of the group. When we lived alone, however, is when we discovered our true selves.

I discovered that I tended not to be self-motivated. I was content to just share my dreams and goals with others and I felt that they had been fulfilled. I realized that I was more comfortable helping others get to where they were going by investing my time and resources but I took a very lax view on my own progress. After living with groups of people for over 25 years, I couldn't buy myself a new pair of shoes without thinking of how it would collectively, affect those around me. I had trouble spending money on myself and constantly felt selfish for wanting something for myself.

Most importantly and tragically, I struggled to have a vibrant relationship with Jesus outside of a group. I discovered that I had somehow believed that God hears my prayers better when other people prayed for/with me and that on many days, I was okay to just stay in bed and not seek God. I believed the most uplifting times were those when people contributed to the God experience (so to speak).

Therein lay my challenge. Were my discoveries in singlehood in discovering my identity causing me to procrastinate (or causing me to wait in peace…. I should explore this thought) marriage?

On some days, I do avoid it entirely while on others I have felt like, "God, marriage is beautiful. Grow me into the person who can be a part of it."

Oh, back to the dinner conversation. In that conversation, I realized that I think of marriage as a cage and that I may never fulfil my purpose within its "boundaries" but would instead revert to God's purpose for *our* marriage as opposed to God's purpose for me.

I just want you to understand that I am in the middle of things believing that I'll come out fine on the other side which may not be where I am when you read this, but here I am.

Regardless, an open space where you and God can sit and discuss life issues is important. He will correct your misguided passions, you will know how much He loves you, and you will know *who* love is. Ultimately, I hope that my chapter on marriage and relationship with God will look like this:

"Who is this coming up from the wilderness leaning on her beloved?" Songs of Solomon 8:5

With Love,
A sis.

CLOSING WORDS

Congratulations, for being sincere and picking up this book because you care that God ought to be involved in every area of your life. You are right to place value on the season of waiting that exists before you meet your future spouse. God cares that you want him closely involved in deciding for your ideal spouse. It is honourable that you desire a godly marriage and you are willing to remain single until you meet the person God has for you.

This book has relayed that it is in the moments when you feel most discontented as a single woman that you need to fully embrace your identity in Christ and stand firm on his promises. It's through the constant use of the Word of God to confront the struggles you encounter during the wait that you are refined. By overcoming anxiety you are able to free your mind to envision a good future while simultaneously enjoying singleness, having laid down all your burdens.

Although we have come to the end of this book, this is not the end of your journey. You've got to keep pressing into God and keep persevering in your faith. You have come this far. Refuse to compromise now. Keep standing on the Word against all odds. I know you understand by now that this book is not a checklist of the things that you ought to do in order for God to bring you a man. It is so much more! In this book, you have learnt how to defeat your biggest enemy right now, anxiety. I've relayed how you can overcome self-condemnation. You are a woman who does not need to feel sorry for yourself or rush the future.

I hope that you will become more content with your current single status and live as a person with hope that never disappoints. More than anything, I pray that you will be fully present to all the moments you experience as a single woman and that you may still stand firm even after encountering so many tests and temptations.

I would love to hear your testimonies of how this book has helped you. I would also be honoured if we could converse about where you are at in your journey so that we could keep each other in check and grow together.

everysinglemomentbook@gmail.com

Antonia Nazombe

@antonianazombe

SALVATION PRAYER

Jesus, I believe in you. I believe you are God and that you left your glory in heaven, and took on flesh. You demonstrated love in its fullest form when you took my sin and died in my place on the cross. Today, I receive your unconditional love, mercy, and grace. Oh Lord, you love me. Today, I have become your daughter and you are my Father. I now belong to your family and I declare you Lord over my life. Give me the ability and grace to know you more. In Jesus's name, Amen.

ACKNOWLEDGEMENTS

Wati, Vanessa and Elita. I've seen you girls do the impossible and you made me believe I could too. Thank you!

To all my girls and our enriched conversations –thank you for loving Jesus, thank you for endorsing purity and thank you for being gracious enough to share life with me. Freda, Tamara, Linley, and Charity. Y'all are a treasure. Thank you for your authenticity. Thank you for doing life with me. I treasure our conversations.

Many others generously read drafts and offered thoughts, sometimes under demanding deadlines. Special thanks to Winnie Mughogho you are a star. "Winstah"...Lol... Thank you for being trustworthy, approachable and genuine. Thank you for your contribution to making this book an excellent work. Timwa Lipenga, you are one of the sweetest people on this entire planet; I am bolder because of you. Elita Chamdimba, this book would not have been possible without your edits on the first-ever draft, you refined this entire book. God bless you! Thank you, Pastor Vincent Chirwa, Martha Chikuni, Yamiko Chamdimba, Roshan Makhole, Bonwell Utonga, Masa Chijere, Dumi Kayiya, Akuzike Zingani, Amanda Nazombe, Ucizi Manda, Charity Nyirenda, and Duwa Gondwe.

To Mr. Smith Likongwe. Thank you for helping me rediscover my love for writing. I was eager to stumble through the entire writing process of this book because you presented the art of writing as a gift made available to everyone, including me.

Dear Dad, I surely find writing easier because of you. Thank you for the good genes. Thank you for leaving a legacy. My dear sisters, Annette and Amanda. Thank you for being genuine with me. You have been more than sisters to me. I look up to you. Va, BFF☺ you literally help me celebrate life. Man, you get excited about everything and that encourages me to aim higher. Thank you. Mummy, thank you for raising me to believe that I can do anything. Thank you for always being supportive. I love you.

Dr. Ellen Chirwa, your testimony has stuck with me since the day you shared it. You fuelled my desire to embrace singleness. Thank you. Blantyre Baptist Church and the Sold Out Bible Study Group, thank you for making great deposits of life-changing knowledge that has led to my spiritual growth. I forever cherish your lessons.

Thank you My FAM Bible Study and Capital City Baptist Church for consistently washing me with the water of the Word!

NOTES

Chapter One

[1] https://tonyevans.org/how-to-repond-to-gods-love/
[2] https://decibel.one/to-the-one-who-feels-lonely-this-valentines/
[3] Matthew 22: 39

Chapter Two

[1] 2 Kings 4: 16
[2] Judges 6:15
[3] http://youtu.be/mtWETAMcytM
[4] John 11: 1-44
[5] http:// m.facebook.com/story.php?story_fbid=1543598345660862&id=146855628668481
[6] John 14:26 KJV

Chapter Three

[1] Isaiah 43:1 ESV
[2] https:// www. merriam-webster.com/dictionary/jerk
[3] https:// www.merriam-webster.com/dictionary/erotic
[4] Psalm 34: 18
[5] Esther 1:1
[6] https://www.josephprince.com/meditate-devo/you-are-highly-favored-because-of-jesus

Chapter Four

[1] 1 John 4:19
[2] https://youtu.be/NjXJWcKxHpY

Chapter Five

[1] Luke 10: 40-42

Chapter Six

[1] Titus 3:5-6

Chapter Seven

[1] Genesis 39: 2;23
[2] 1 Corinthians 10:13
[3] Psalm 25:3
[4] Philippians 4:4
[5] James 1:2-4
[6] Genesis 45: 4-8
[7] Romans 12:2 MSG

Chapter Eight

[1] 1 Corinthians 6:18; Ephesian 5:3

Chapter Nine

[1] Proverbs 10:22
[2] Ephesians 5: 22-33; 1 Peter 3: 7
[3] Acts 10: 38
[4] Psalm 23:6
[5] 1 Corinthians 15: 10

Chapter Ten

[1] Malachi 3: 16
[2] https://biblehub.com/commentaries/daniel/1-8.htm
[3] https://www.biblestudytools.com/dictionary/ruth/
[4] Matthew 1: 5
[5] https://www.psychologytoday.com/us/basics/self-talk

Chapter Eleven

[1] Leviticus 26:8; Deuteronomy 32:30

Made in the USA
Las Vegas, NV
24 December 2025

37775532R00090